Disability and Human Rights in the Workplace

A CLV Special Report

Adelyn L. Bowland

B.A., LL.B., LL.M.

THOMSON

CARSWELL

National Library of Canada Cataloguing in Publication

Bowland, Adelyn
  Disability and human rights in the workplace / Adelyn L. Bowland.

(CLV special report)
Includes bibliographical references and index.
ISBN 0-459-28293-X

  1. People with disabilities--Employment--Law and legislation--Canada. 2. Discrimination in employment--Law and legislation--Canada. I. Title. II. Series: CLV special report series.

KE3254.B69 2003   344.7101'59   C2003-905858-1
KF3464.B69 2003

THOMSON

━━━━━━━━★━━━━━━━━ ™

CARSWELL

One Corporate Plaza	Customer Relations
2075 Kennedy Road	Toronto 1-416-609-3800
Toronto, Ontario	Elsewhere in Canada/U.S. 1-800-387-5164
M1T 3V4	Fax 1-416-298-5094
	World Wide Web: http://www.carswell.com
	E-mail: orders@carswell.com

About the Author

Adelyn Bowland is a human rights mediator in Toronto. Called to the Ontario Bar in 1980, she has worked in human rights law and related areas for over twenty years. As co-counsel for the Government of Canada, she was involved in the "rape shield" case of *Seaboyer v. R.*, before the Supreme Court of Canada. She is also a writer and is the author of the *Annotated Ontario Human Rights Code* for Carswell. She received her legal training (LL.B. and LL.M.) at Osgoode Hall Law School, York University.

Brief Contents

Contents

◆
INTRODUCTION

Disability complaints to Canadian human rights commissions have increased dramatically in recent years. Across Canada, human rights commissions report that allegations of discrimination based on disability account for the largest number of complaints. This ranges from 65% of complaints in Ontario to 27% in Nova Scotia.[1]

In a very general sense, human rights law includes the equality provisions of the *Charter of Rights and Freedoms*, part of the *Constitution*, as well as the provincial and federal human rights statutes. In the employment context, the main difference between the *Charter* and provincial human rights legislation is that the *Charter* only applies to government employers, while provincial human rights legislation applies to both government and other employers. Provincial and federal human rights statutes are considered quasi-constitutional; thus, they take precedence over any other statute, except the *Constitution*. This means they determine the interpretation of all employment legislation.

This publication surveys non-*Charter* human rights law and policies relating to disability at both the provincial (territorial) and federal levels, except for Quebec. The names of the statutes vary slightly as do the statutory provisions; however, they are interpreted in a similar way because of the purpose they have in common.[2] In the employment context, this purpose is to support the employment of disabled employees and require employers to accommodate them to the point of undue hardship.

Human rights statutes are administered by human rights commissions, except for British Columbia. Decisions of tribunals[3] and courts define the law. However, it is the policies of the Human Rights Commissions which define the Commissions' expectations of employers as well as the investigation of human rights complaints.[4]

The purpose of this book is to explain the human rights obligations of Canadian employers, employees and unions in dealing with disability in the workplace with respect to hiring, employment and dismissal. While there are overlaps with legislation governing workers' compensation , employment standards and health and safety, human rights law must be followed, irrespective of due diligence concerning other laws governing employment.[5]

This book is divided into eight main sections: reasonable accommodation and undue hardship; disability defined; the duty of the employee, employer and union; medical issues, suitable alternative employment; absence from work; reasonable accommodation and substance abuse; and discharge.

ENDNOTES

[1] The one exception to this is the Yukon. The human rights commission there indicates that sex discrimination accounts for the largest number of complaints, followed by disability. Alberta Human Rights Commission, *Annual Review* 2001–2002; Canadian Human Rights Commission, *2002 Annual* Report; Nova Scotia Human Rights Commission, *Annual Report 2000–2001*; Manitoba Human Rights Commission *Annual Report* 2001; Newfoundland & Labrador Human Rights Commission, *Report for* 2002–2001; New Brunswick Human Rights Commission, *Annual Report* 2001–2002; Ontario Human Rights Commission, *Year End Results 2002*; Prince Edward Island Human Rights Commission, *19th Fiscal Report* 2001–2002; Saskatchewan Human Rights Commission, *2002–2003 Annual Report*; Yukon Human Rights Commission, *Report on Activities April 1, 1999–April 1, 2001*. British Columbia does not have a human rights commission. This publication does not include Quebec law.

[2] See Appendix A for a list of human rights statutes.

[3] Except for British Columbia, most human rights complaints are made to Human Rights Commissions. The Commission may then refer the complaint to a human rights tribunal. In British Columbia, human rights complaints are made directly to the human rights tribunal. In a unionized workplace, these complaints may ordinarily be launched in a grievance, where they are heard by labour arbitrators.

[4] Only British Columbia has no Human Rights Commission.

[5] Barriers to accessibility for those with physical impairments, for instance hearing difficulties or the use of wheelchair, will not be addressed here. Nor will employer obligations relating to workers' compensation, employment contracts or labour unions.

♦

CHAPTER 1

REASONABLE ACCOMMODATION AND UNDUE HARDSHIP

- Cost
- Size of Business
- Interests of Co-workers
- Health and Safety
- Contracts
- Disruption of Operations
- How much Hardship is Undue?

Employers are required to accommodate employees protected under human rights statutes; they are required to provide what is referred to in human rights law as "reasonable accommodation". This duty extends to employees on the basis of several grounds; for instance: religion, disability and gender (particularly pregnancy.)

When an employee asks for accommodation of a need, the employer is expected to respond with flexibility. But there are limits with respect to this flexibility; the employer must not experience "undue hardship", which is to be assessed on an objective, rather than impressionistic basis.

Several factors are relevant in determining undue hardship.

- Costs to the employer,
- Size of the operation,
- Interchangeability of the workforce and facilities,
- Disruption of a collective agreement,
- Disruption of operations,
- Rests of co-workers and
- Safety of the disabled employee, co-workers, patients, customers and the general public.

Factors considered irrelevant to the assessment of undue hardship are:

- Customer or public preference.
- Discriminatory objections.
- Compliance with other legislation.
- Threatened grievances.[1]

Cost

Often the most important factor to an employer is the cost of accommodation. To constitute undue hardship, costs must be so significant they would substantially affect productivity or efficiency. In any event, the employer is expected to explore cost-reduced alternatives.[2] The employer should also explore whether there are outside sources of funding, tax exemptions, grants, subsidies or other possible gains.[3]

Size of the Business

The size of the business relates to the interchangeability of the workforce and facilities. Generally, a larger employer will be under a higher duty to accommodate a disability; the larger operation gives the employer increased flexibility and financial resources. However, a large but highly specialized employer may have more difficulty accommodating a disabled employee.

Interests of Co-Workers

In any type of accommodation, it is necessary to balance interests. The most obvious balancing is between the interests of the disabled employee and the employer. However, the interests of co-workers, their morale and rights, are important as well.

The issue of the morale of co-workers is a tricky one. Clearly, discriminatory attitudes of co-workers are irrelevant. However, if accommodation would require co-workers to increase their overtime or be available on call to assist a disabled employee with heavy lifting, this would be relevant.

Accommodation of a disabled employee should not be discriminatory towards a co-worker and should take into account the rights of co-workers, as determined by the collective agreement and legislation determining workers' compensation, employment standards as well as employee health and safety. However, an option for accommodation should only be rejected if it causes a substantial interference with the rights of co-workers.[4]

Health and Safety

The assessment of health and safety is based on the likelihood of the risk being actualized and the extent of the injury or damage which could occur. Standards of safety should not be uncompromisingly stringent and where the risk is solely to the disabled employee, the degree of acceptable risk is greater. Assessing the risks and the appropriate level of safety is the responsibility of the employer and may include the employer's own direct experience of the employee's ability to deal with the risks. Overall, the risks normally assumed by the employer, employees, the industry, customers, clients and the public are all relevant.[5]

Contracts

The Supreme Court of Canada has indicated that human rights legislation prevails over contracts.[6] Thus, ordinarily, the requirements of the duty to accommodate prevail over the terms of the collective agreement, although the extent of the disruption of the collective agreement is relevant.[7] The Supreme Court of Canada has also indicated that parties cannot contract out of the provisions of human rights legislation.[8] This means that, in terms of employer agreements with individual employees, employers cannot require employees to forego their rights under human rights legislation. Nor can employees voluntarily contract out of these rights. Thus, restrictive conditions, last chance agreements and minutes of settlement relating to disability are subject to the duty to accommodate.[9]

Recently, the Supreme Court of Canada stated that human rights legislation applies to probationary employees. This means the employer is under a duty to accommodate a disabled probationary employee.[10]

Disruption of Operations

Some of the matters dealt with above can cause disruption of business operations. To constitute undue hardship, the potential disruption must affect some essential aspect of the operation. Business inconvenience is irrelevant.[11]

How Much Hardship Is "Undue"?

It is clear that the employer is expected to accept hardship in accommodating a disabled employee. But the hardship should not be "undue". Gauging how much hardship is "undue" is difficult. It would appear that the standard is very high, that the employer is expected to investigate all possible options to accommodate a disabled employee, including absence from work—either full-time or part-time—for an extended length of time. This far surpasses minor inconvenience.[12]

The Alberta Human Rights Commission indicates the following are possible options:

- Purchase or modify tools, equipment or aids.
- Alter the premises to make them accessible.
- Alter aspects of the job, such as job duties.
- Offer a flexible work schedule.
- Offer a rehabilitation program.
- Allow time off for recuperation.
- Transfer the disabled employee to a different job.
- Hire an assistant.
- Adjust policies.[13]

In each case, the relevant factors will vary, as will their importance. It is not possible to formulate a rule because each assessment must be individual. What is possible for a government employer with entire departments and volumes of information available to it may not be possible for a small private company required to make decisions amid operational pressures posed by scheduling, customer relations, profitability and legal liability. It is a matter of considering the harm to the disabled employee caused by not implementing the accommodation and the hardship (mainly to the employer, but also to co-workers, the union and the public) caused by its implementation.[14]

ENDNOTES

[1] See Appendix B, Alberta Human Rights Commission, *The Duty to Accommodate* and Ontario Human Rights Commission, *Disability and the Duty to Accommodate.*

[2] *British Columbia (Public Service Employee Relations Commission) v. B.C.G.E.U.*, [1999] 3 S.C.R. 3, 1999 CarswellBC 1907, 1999 CarswellBC 1908, [1999] S.C.J. No. 46, 99 C.L.L.C. 230-028, [1999]

10 W.W.R. 1, 176 D.L.R. (4th) 1, 244 N.R. 145, 66 B.C.L.R. (3d) 253, 127 B.C.A.C. 161, 207 W.A.C. 161, 46 C.C.E.L. (2d) 206, 35 C.H.R.R. D/257, 68 C.R.R. (2d) 1, 7 B.H.R.C. 437 (S.C.C.)

[3] See Appendix B, Ontario Human Rights Commission, *Disability and the Duty to Accommodate* and Alberta Human Rights Commission, *Duty to Accommodate.*

[4] The rights of co-workers are dealt with in more detail below in Chapter 5. Suitable Alternative Employment — Seniority, Collective Agreement.

[5] *British Columbia (Public Service Employee Relations Commission) v. B.C.G.E.U.*, [1999] 3 S.C.R. 3, 1999 CarswellBC 1907, 1999 CarswellBC 1908, [1999] S.C.J. No. 46, 99 C.L.L.C. 230-028, [1999] 10 W.W.R. 1, 176 D.L.R. (4th) 1, 244 N.R. 145, 66 B.C.L.R. (3d) 253, 127 B.C.A.C. 161, 207 W.A.C. 161, 46 C.C.E.L. (2d) 206, 35 C.H.R.R. D/257, 68 C.R.R. (2d) 1, 7 B.H.R.C. 437 (S.C.C.); *British Columbia (Superintendent of Motor Vehicles) v. British Columbia (Council of Human Rights)* (1999), [1999] 3 S.C.R. 868, 1999 CarswellBC 2730, 1999 CarswellBC 2731, [1999] S.C.J. No. 73, [2000] 1 W.W.R. 565, 47 M.V.R. (3d) 167, 249 N.R. 45, 70 B.C.L.R. (3d) 215, 181 D.L.R. (4th) 385, 36 C.H.R.R. D/129, 131 B.C.A.C. 280, 214 W.A.C. 280 (S.C.C.); *Wabush Mines v. Power* (1997), 1997 CarswellNfld 202, 153 D.L.R. (4th) 739, 157 Nfld. & P.E.I.R. 144, 486 A.P.R. 144, 30 C.H.R.R. D/87, 98 C.L.L.C. 230-005, 33 C.C.E.L. (2d) 4 (Nfld. C.A.) See below, Chapter 5. Suitable Alternative Employment — Assumption of Risk.

[6] *N.A.P.E. v. Newfoundland*, 134 D.L.R. (4th) 1, 1996 CarswellNfld 133, 1996 CarswellNfld 133F, [1996] S.C.J. No. 54, 196 N.R. 212, 39 Admin. L.R. (2d) 1, 140 Nfld. & P.E.I.R. 63, 438 A.P.R. 63, 96 C.L.L.C. 230-023, [1996] 2 S.C.R. 3, 28 C.H.R.R. D/224, [1996] L.V.I. 2757-1 (S.C.C.)

[7] *Chambly (Commission scolaire régionale) v. Bergevin*, 21 Admin. L.R. (2d) 169, 1994 CarswellQue 78, 1994 CarswellQue 114, 4 C.C.E.L. (2d) 165, 169 N.R. 281, 94 C.L.L.C. 17,023, 62 Q.A.C. 241, [1994] 2 S.C.R. 525, 115 D.L.R. (4th) 609, 22 C.H.R.R. D/1 (S.C.C.); *Renaud v. Central Okanagan School District No. 23*, 141 N.R. 185, 1992 CarswellBC 257, 1992 CarswellBC 910, [1992] 6 W.W.R. 193, 95 D.L.R. (4th) 577, 24 W.A.C. 245, 92 C.L.L.C. 17,032, 71 B.C.L.R. (2d) 145, [1992] 2 S.C.R. 970, 13 B.C.A.C. 245, 16 C.H.R.R. D/425 (S.C.C.)

[8] *N.A.P.E. v. Newfoundland, supra* note 6

[9] For example, see *Sobeys v. U.F.C.W., Local 175* (2002), 2002 CarswellOnt 3862, 105 L.A.C. (4th) 346 (Ont. Arb. Bd.). For more details, see below, Chapter 6. Absence from Work — Last Chance Agreements; Chapter 7 Reasonable Accommodation and Substance Abuse; Chapter 8 Discharge

[10] *Parry Sound (District) Welfare Administration Board v. O.P.S.E.U., Local 324* 2003 CarswellOnt 3500, 2003 SCC 42 (S.C.C.). See also *Canada Post Corp. v. C.U.P.W.* (1998), 73 L.A.C. (4th) 15, 1998 CarswellNat 2501 (Can. Arb. Bd.); *Clarke v. Country Garden Florists* (1996), 96 C.L.L.C. 230-018, 26 C.H.R.R. D/24 (Nfld. Bd. of Inquiry). But see the limitations in *Dominion Castings Ltd. v. U.S.W.A., Local 9393* (1996), 1996 CarswellOnt 4017 (Ont. Arb. Bd.)

[11] See Appendix B, Ontario Human Rights Commission, *Disability and the Duty to Accommodate.*

[12] *British Columbia (Public Service Employee Relations Commission) v. B.C.G.E.U.*, 35 C.H.R.R. D/257, [1999] 3 S.C.R. 3, 1999 CarswellBC 1907, 1999 CarswellBC 1908, [1999] S.C.J. No. 46, 99 C.L.L.C. 230-028, [1999] 10 W.W.R. 1, 176 D.L.R. (4th) 1, 244 N.R. 145, 66 B.C.L.R. (3d) 253, 127 B.C.A.C. 161, 207 W.A.C. 161, 46 C.C.E.L. (2d) 206, 68 C.R.R. (2d) 1, 7 B.H.R.C. 437 (S.C.C.); *Parisien v. Ottawa-Carlton Transit Comm.*, 2003 CHRT 10 (Can. Human Rights Trib.)

[13] See Appendix B, Alberta Human Rights Commission, *Duty to Accommodate*

[14] *British Columbia (Public Service Employee Relations Commission) v. B.C.G.E.U.*, 35 C.H.R.R. D/257, [1999] 3 S.C.R. 3, 1999 CarswellBC 1907, 1999 CarswellBC 1908, [1999] S.C.J. No. 46, 99 C.L.L.C. 230-028, [1999] 10 W.W.R. 1, 176 D.L.R. (4th) 1, 244 N.R. 145, 66 B.C.L.R. (3d) 253, 127 B.C.A.C. 161, 207 W.A.C. 161, 46 C.C.E.L. (2d) 206, 68 C.R.R. (2d) 1, 7 B.H.R.C. 437 (S.C.C.); *Oak Bay Marina Ltd. v. British Columbia (Human Rights Commission)*, 2002 BCCA 495,2002 CarswellBC 2057, [2002] B.C.J. No. 2029, 5 B.C.L.R. (4th) 115, [2002] 10 W.W.R. 399, 217 D.L.R. (4th) 747, 20 C.C.E.L. (3d) 1, 2002 C.L.L.C. 230-038, 172 B.C.A.C. 267, 282 W.A.C. 267, 43 C.H.R.R. D/487 (B.C. C.A.); *U.N.A., Local 33 v. Capital Health Authority*, 2003 CarswellAlta 611, 2003 ABQB 375 (Alta. Q.B.)

◆

CHAPTER 2

DISABILITY DEFINED

- Generally
- List of Conditions
- Diagnosed Cause
- Not Just Present Disability
- Mental Disability
- Summary

Generally

Disability is defined broadly in the legislation of each jurisdiction and includes both physical and mental illness. In the past, human rights law has been based on two alternative approaches: whether the condition fell within a list of conditions defined as disabilities or whether there was a diagnosed medical cause. Recently the Supreme Court of Canada defined a new approach—that is, whether the condition detrimentally affects the employee in the workplace or limits full participation in society.[1]

List of Conditions

Some tribunals and courts have placed primary emphasis on the condition or state of the individual (injury, illness or birth defect).[2] This approach tends to rely on whether the disability falls within a list of medical problems. Certain physical conditions are without exception included, such as AIDS, cancer and alcohol or drug addiction.[3] Because substance abuse has loomed large in human rights complaints, several human rights commissions have issued policies with respect to alcohol and drug addiction.[4]

Ailments, or temporary conditions, such as a cold or flu, are excluded from the list.[5] A recent Newfoundland and Labrador Court of Appeal decision indicated that recurring ailments are not covered. However, the Ontario Human Rights Commission includes conditions which are episodic, minor or temporary in nature if they result in unfair treatment because of the perception of a disability.[6]

Diagnosed Cause

The "list" approach can be confounding when considering such diagnoses as allergies, which have been included and excluded, depending on their cause.[7] Nor does this approach assist in dealing with obesity, which will be excluded unless caused by bodily injury, a birth defect or illness.[8]

Some tribunals have found that the diagnosed cause is not definitive of whether a condition is a handicap under human rights legislation. Thus, for instance:

- Gradual onset work-related injuries are not excluded from the definition of handicap.[9]
- The heart condition, lone atrial fibrillation, is a handicap even though its cause is unknown.[10]

Not Just Present Disabilities

Not just present medical conditions are included in the definition of disability. The broadest definition of handicap relates to employer perceptions. The underlying concern here is to prevent discrimination based on negative perceptions of employee effectiveness relating to a present, past or anticipated future medical condition.[11] This emphasizes not the existence of a disability, but the perception of the employer and is difficult to prove.[12]

Mental Disabilities

A recent study of 180 companies by Watson Wyatt Canada indicated that 79% of respondents ranked psychological conditions as the leading cause of short-term disabilities and 73% ranked them as the main cause of long-term disabilities.[13] Mental disabilities are included in the definition of disability in human rights law and are the most difficult for both employers and employees. This is largely because of the stigma attached to all types of mental disabilities, whether learning disabilities, intellectual limitations, psychological difficulties or substance abuse. This means that both employees and employers find it difficult to even discuss the problem, let alone deal with accommodation. People often make assumptions about mental disabilities which hamper employment relations; for instance, it may be assumed that an employee who has been successfully treated for Post-Traumatic-Stress-Syndrome will have a relapse. Nevertheless, employers have a duty to accommodate a mental disability; this may true even if it is not disclosed by the employee.[14]

This puts the onus on the employer to develop human resource programs to encourage disabled employees to seek assistance and to educate both managers and co-workers. Nonetheless, the accommodation of mental disabilities, particularly psychological disorders and substance abuse, often requires the facilities and financial resources of a larger employer if it is necessary to actively supervise and monitor the employee.[15]

Summary

Ailments and short term conditions are not ordinarily considered disabilities under human rights legislation. However, there is protection for any physical or mental condition which detrimentally affects the employee in the workplace or limits participation in society. Moreover, where an employee experiences negative treatment because of a perceived present or future disability, this is also relevant. This very broad definition of disability requires a broad spectrum of human resource policies and administrative practices to identify the disability and assess related performance issues.

ENDNOTES

[1] *Québec (Commission des droits de la personne & des droits de la jeunesse) v. Montréal (Ville)*, [2000] 1 S.C.R. 665, 2000 CarswellQue 649, 2000 CarswellQue 650, [2000] S.C.J. No. 24, 2000 SCC 27, 2000 C.L.L.C. 230-020, 185 D.L.R. (4th) 385, 50 C.C.E.L. (2d) 247, [2000] L.V.I. 3115-1, 253 N.R. 107, 74 C.R.R. (2d) 80, 37 C.H.R.R. D/271 (S.C.C.)

[2] *Kearsley v. Ontario (Human Rights Commission)* (2002), 2002 CarswellOnt 5050, 42 C.H.R.R. D/304 (Ont. Bd. of Inquiry)

[3] See *Entrop v. Imperial Oil Ltd.* (2000), 2 C.C.E.L. (3d) 19, 2000 CarswellOnt 2525, [2000] O.J. No. 2689, 189 D.L.R. (4th) 14, 50 O.R. (3d) 18, 2000 C.L.L.C. 230-037, 137 O.A.C. 15, 37 C.H.R.R. D/481 (Ont. C.A.); *Canadian Civil Liberties Assn. v. Toronto Dominion*

Bank, 1998 CarswellNat 1352, 1998 CarswellNat 2708, [1998] F.C.J. No. 1036, 98 C.L.L.C. 230-030, 229 N.R. 135, 163 D.L.R. (4th) 193, 38 C.C.E.L. (2d) 8, 32 C.H.R.R. D/261, [1998] 4 F.C. 205, 154 F.T.R. 101 (note) (Fed. C.A.)

[4] All of them are contained in Appendix B, as are the following: Ontario Human Rights Commission, *Disability and the Duty to Accommodate*; Alberta Human Rights Commission, *Duty to Accommodate* and see below, Chapter 7. Reasonable Accommodation and Substance Abuse.

[5] *Québec (Commission des droits de la personne & des droits de la jeunesse) v. Montréal (Ville)*, [2000] 1 S.C.R. 665, 2000 CarswellQue 649, 2000 CarswellQue 650, [2000] S.C.J. No. 24, 2000 SCC 27, 2000 C.L.L.C. 230-020, 185 D.L.R. (4th) 385, 50 C.C.E.L. (2d) 247, [2000] L.V.I. 3115-1, 253 N.R. 107, 74 C.R.R. (2d) 80, 37 C.H.R.R. D/271 (S.C.C.)

[6] *Newfoundland (Human Rights Commission) v. Health Care Corp. of St. John's* 2003 CarswellNfld 54, 2003 NLCA 13, 223 Nfld. & P.E.I.R. 1, 666 A.P.R. 1 (N.L. C.A.); see also *Bonner v. Ontario (Minister of Health)* (1992), 16 C.H.R.R. D/485, 92 C.L.L.C. 17,019 (Ont. Bd. of Inquiry); Appendix B Ontario Human Rights Commission, *Disability and the Duty to Accommodate*. In Saskatchewan, a Human Rights Board of Inquiry recently found that severe whiplash is a handicap. *Shirley v. Eecol Electric (Sask.) Ltd.* (2001), 2001 CarswellSask 255, 2001 C.L.L.C. 230-021, 39 C.H.R.R. D/168 (Sask. Bd. of Inquiry)

[7] *Ouimette v. Lily Cups Ltd.* (1990), 12 C.H.R.R. D/19, 90 C.L.L.C. 17,019 (Ont. Bd. of Inquiry); *Morgoch v. Ottawa (City)* (1989), 11 C.H.R.R. D/80, 89 C.L.L.C. 17,026 (Ont. Bd. of Inquiry)

[8] *Horton v. Niagara (Regional Municipality)* (1987), 9 C.H.R.R. D/4611, 1987 CarswellOnt 921, 19 C.C.E.L. 259, 88 C.L.L.C. 17,004 (Ont. Bd. of Inquiry)

[9] *Ontario Jockey Club v. S.E.I.U., Local 528* (2001), 151 O.A.C. 375, 2001 CarswellOnt 3904, 41 C.H.R.R. D/361 (Ont. Div. Ct.)

[10] *Kearsley v. Ontario (Human Rights Commission)* (2002), 2002 CarswellOnt 5050, 42 C.H.R.R. D/304 (Ont. Bd. of Inquiry)

[11] *Québec (Commission des droits de la personne & des droits de la jeunesse) v. Montréal (Ville)*, [2000] 1 S.C.R. 665, 2000 CarswellQue 649, 2000 CarswellQue 650, [2000] S.C.J. No. 24, 2000 SCC 27, 2000 C.L.L.C. 230-020, 185 D.L.R. (4th) 385, 50 C.C.E.L. (2d) 247, [2000] L.V.I. 3115-1, 253 N.R. 107, 74 C.R.R. (2d) 80, 37 C.H.R.R. D/271 (S.C.C.); *Marcil v. Vantage Contracting Ltd.* (June 5, 2003), No. 6076

(Alta. Human Rights Panel); *Parisien v. Ottawa-Carlton Transit Comm.*, 2003 CHRT 10 (Can. Human Rights Trib.)

[12] *Middlemiss v. Norske Canada Ltd.*, 2002 CarswellBC 2014, 2002 C.L.L.C. 230-024, 2002 BCHRT 5 (B.C. Human Rights Trib.); *Newfoundland (Human Rights Commission) v. Health Care Corp. of St. John's* (2001), 2001 CarswellNfld 98, 199 Nfld. & P.E.I.R. 268, 600 A.P.R. 268, 40 C.H.R.R. D/101, 19 C.C.E.L. (3d) 111 (Nfld. T.D.), affirmed 2003 CarswellNfld 54, 2003 NLCA 13, 223 Nfld. & P.E.I.R. 1, 666 A.P.R. 1 (N.L. C.A.); *Martin v. Carter Chevrolet Oldsmobile*, 2002 C.L.L.C. 230-020, 2001 CarswellBC 3159, 2001 BCHRT 37, 41 C.H.R.R. D/88 (B.C. Human Rights Trib.) *Pacholko v. Patel* (2001), 2002 C.L.L.C. 230-004, 2001 CarswellSask 859 (Sask. Bd. of Inquiry)

[13] Galt & Harding. "No safety in the numbers." *Globe and Mail* June 18, 2003

[14] *Parisien v. Ottawa-Carlton Transit Comm.*, 2003 CHRT 10 (Can. Human Rights Trib.); *Ottawa Civic Hospital v. O.N.A.* (1995), 1995 CarswellOnt 1438, 48 L.A.C. (4th) 388 (Ont. Arb. Bd.)

[15] *Oak Bay Marina Ltd. v. British Columbia (Human Rights Commission)*, 2002 BCCA 495, 2002 CarswellBC 2057, [2002] B.C.J. No. 2029, 5 B.C.L.R. (4th) 115, [2002] 10 W.W.R. 399, 217 D.L.R. (4th) 747, 20 C.C.E.L. (3d) 1, 2002 C.L.L.C. 230-038, 172 B.C.A.C. 267, 282 W.A.C. 267, 43 C.H.R.R. D/487 (B.C. C.A.)*; Ottawa Civic Hospital v. O.N.A.* (1995), 1995 CarswellOnt 1438, 48 L.A.C. (4th) 388 (Ont. Arb. Bd.); *Bonner v. Ontario (Minister of Health)* (1992), 16 C.H.R.R. D/485, 92 C.L.L.C. 17,019 (Ont. Bd. of Inquiry); Kyriakopoulos., S. "Accommodating Mental and Psychological Disabilities" and Lynk, M., "Accommodation, Disability and the Unionized Workplace" in *Human Rights in the Unionized Workplace*, C.B.A.O., Continuing Legal Education: 2001 and see below, Chapter 3. The Duty of the Employee, Employer and Union

◆
CHAPTER 3

THE DUTY OF THE EMPLOYEE, EMPLOYER AND UNION

- Hiring
- On the job
  - Request for accommodation
  - Review of options
- Summary

Not only do employers have responsibilities under human rights legislation; but disabled employees and unions also have responsibilities. All the involved parties must work together in a constructive, flexible fashion.[1]

Hiring

Human rights law affects the entire process of hiring new employees. The employer's duties start when the job description is written and continue through the interview and selection process.

The employer's first step in meeting human rights obligations is to have job descriptions for all positions. This is absolutely necessary with respect to dealing with disability in the workplace. The job description should have a detailed list of all the duties of the position, differentiating the essential from the non-essential. "Non-essential duties" have been defined as incidental tasks or tasks performed regularly but rarely. "Essential duties" have been defined alternatively as "core" duties or as most of the duties.[2]

Where there are job requirements which limit potential applicants on the basis of a disability (for instance, with respect to eyesight or strength) the requirement should not be set above what is absolutely necessary for the essential duties of the job. Any limitation with respect to disability must be a *bona fide* occupational requirement. Minimum or maximum height or weight restrictions are unlawful.[3]

As important as the job description are the job advertisement and the application form. A job advertisement should reflect the essential duties of the job description. In terms of the application form, unless the requirement not to have a particular disability is a *bona fide* occupational qualification, questions with respect to disabilities should be excluded. Nor should the application form contain questions regarding the following:

- Health problems or limitations
- Hospitalization
- Medical tests
- Therapy
- Medication
- Drug and/or alcohol consumption
- Previous injuries
- Disabilities
- Medical history
- Membership in a medical or patient association (for instance, Alcoholics Anonymous)
- Work injuries
- Claims for workers' compensation
- Disability-related needs[4]

As part of the selection process, the employer may test for skills related to the essential duties of the job. Here, the employer is under a duty to accommodate learning disabilities related to the testing. With respect to competitions based on the merit principle, the employer should attempt to find accommodation which permits the disabled applicant to compete on an equal footing with other candidates. This must be balanced against fairness to other candidates.[5]

At the job interview, the rules are different. An employer may ask whether an applicant has any disability-related needs that would require accommodation to enable him or her to perform the essential duties of the job.[6] However, an Ontario Board of Inquiry (Human Rights) has decided that job applicants have no duty to disclose a disability.[7]

On the Job

On the job, sometimes the employer will be aware of the need to accommodate an employee's disability because the disability has resulted from a work injury. Other times, the employer will only know because the employer asks for accommodation of the disability.

Request for Accommodation

With respect to a request for accommodation, the Alberta and Ontario Commissions have detailed policies, as did the former British Columbia Commission. These policies state that the employee need not provide a diagnosis or information about medical treatment, but should indicate their needs and limitations caused by the disability, preferably in writing with support from healthcare specialists, where appropriate.[8]

The Alberta Commission indicates the employee should provide a written statement from their healthcare provider regarding the following:

- Prognosis for full or partial recovery.
- Fitness to return to work.
- Fitness to perform specific components of the pre-injury job.
- Likely duration of the restrictions following a return to work.

Is an employer under a duty to accommodate an employee who does not request accommodation? In limited situations, yes. Sometimes people can't disclose or communicate their needs because of the nature of their disability.

While employers are not expected to diagnose disabilities, they need to be alert to disabilities which are less obvious, such as substance abuse and mental disabilities.

For this reason, employers should:

- Provide a range of opportunities to address performance issues on an individualized basis.
- Practice progressive performance management and discipline.
- Develop employee assistance supports, particularly those which target psychological issues.
- Develop disability management programs to track the reasons employees take sick leaves, personal days off and casual absences.
- Inform all employees that a disability-related assessment or accommodation can be provided as an option to address performance issues.
- Train managers to take note when an employee is showing signs of distress and consider whether the problem is a psychological disability or substance abuse.[9]

Review of Options

Where the workplace is unionized, the union should be included in the discussions and must not impede the employer's efforts to provide accommodation. Apart from this, unions have a general duty to accommodate disabled employees, with respect to the negotiation of the collective agreement, for instance. In any event, whatever its terms, the collective agreement does not override the union's duty to accommodate, unless the accommodation would cause substantial interference with the rights of other employees or the operation of the employer's business.[10]

A disabled employee is not required to originate a solution to the situation or identify a job that he or she is capable of performing.[11] However, an employee must actively co-operate with the employer and/or union in the investigation of the possible options for accommodation. According to the Alberta Human Rights Commission, the employee, or the employee's medical advisor, should have suggestions as to possible methods of accommodation and indicate how long accommodation would be required, if this is known.[12]

Less than full accommodation may be reasonable in some situations.[13] Employees seeking accommodation on the basis of disability must be flexible; they cannot expect perfection and must explain their rejection of proposed accommodation. Nor can an employee refuse reasonable solutions on the ground that the alternative which they favour will not cause the employer undue hardship.[14] If a proposal that would be reasonable in all the circumstances is turned down, the employer's duty is discharged.[15]

Within this framework, the employee, the employer and, in a unionized environment, the union, must discuss possible options for accommodation. However, it is the employer who should take the lead, since it is has the best information about the workplace and is the most aware of the available employment options. Neither the union nor the employee are in the best position to demonstrate whether positions are available, what the essential duties are or whether modifications to these duties could be made. In any event, if an employer is unable to offer any type of accommodation, it should provide to the employee details that justify the refusal to accommodate.[16]

Summary

The duty of the employer to accommodate disabilities under human rights legislation begins even before the job interview. It begins with the job description and the determination of essential and non-essential job duties. The job advertisement, application form and selection process must all conform to human rights obligations.

When a request for accommodation is made, the employee should identify their needs and limitations relating to the disability. But some mental disabilities make it difficult for the affected employee to seek accommodation, yet the employer may still be under a duty to accommodate. In either case, the basis of effective accommodation of the disability is a broad spectrum of human resources policies which clarify job duties, provide progressive performance management, train managers in human rights and provide employee assistance programs.

The employee must co-operate with the employer in reviewing options to accommodate and, in a unionized environment, discussions must include the union. Nonetheless, the onus is on the employer because it has the best information about the workplace and the available job options.

ENDNOTES

[1] *Renaud v. Central Okanagan School District No. 23*, [1992] 2 S.C.R. 970, 1992 CarswellBC 257, 1992 CarswellBC 910, [1992] 6 W.W.R. 193, 95 D.L.R. (4th) 577, 24 W.A.C. 245, 92 C.L.L.C. 17,032, 141 N.R. 185, 71 B.C.L.R. (2d) 145, 13 B.C.A.C. 245, 16 C.H.R.R. D/425 (S.C.C.)

[2] B.C. Human Rights Comission, *The Duty to Accommodate; Hamilton (City) Hydro-Electric Commission v. I.B.E.W., Local 138* (1997), 1997 CarswellOnt 1533 (Ont. Arb. Bd.); *O.P.S.E.U. V. O.E.C.T.A.* (1996), 1996 CarswellOnt 5446, [1997] L.V.I. 2842-5 (Ont. Arb. Bd.); *U.F.C.W., Locals 1175 & 633 v. Community Nursing Home – Port Hope*, 1996 CarswellOnt 5429, [1996] L.V.I. 2809-7 (Ont. Arb. Bd.); See the following publications from Carswell's *Best Practices* series: *Performance Management* and *HR Forms Toolkit* and *Termination*.

[3] *British Columbia (Public Service Employee Relations Commission) v. B.C.G.E.U.*, [1999] 3 S.C.R. 3, 1999 CarswellBC 1907, 1999 CarswellBC 1908, [1999] S.C.J. No. 46, 99 C.L.L.C. 230-028, [1999] 10 W.W.R. 1, 176 D.L.R. (4th) 1, 244 N.R. 145, 66 B.C.L.R. (3d) 253,

127 B.C.A.C. 161, 207 W.A.C. 161, 46 C.C.E.L. (2d) 206, 35 C.H.R.R. D/257, 68 C.R.R. (2d) 1, 7 B.H.R.C. 437 (S.C.C.); *British Columbia (Superintendent of Motor Vehicles) v. British Columbia (Council of Human Rights)* (1999), [1999] 3 S.C.R. 868, 1999 CarswellBC 2730, 1999 CarswellBC 2731, [1999] S.C.J. No. 73, [2000] 1 W.W.R. 565, 47 M.V.R. (3d) 167, 249 N.R. 45, 70 B.C.L.R. (3d) 215, 181 D.L.R. (4th) 385, 36 C.H.R.R. D/129, 131 B.C.A.C. 280, 214 W.A.C. 280 (S.C.C.); *Wabush Mines v. Power* (1997), 1997 CarswellNfld 202, 153 D.L.R. (4th) 739, 157 Nfld. & P.E.I.R. 144, 486 A.P.R. 144, 30 C.H.R.R. D/87, 98 C.L.L.C. 230-005, 33 C.C.E.L. (2d) 4 (Nfld. C.A.); New Brunswick Human Rights Commission, *Employment Application Forms and other Pre-employment Inquiries;* Ontario Human Rights Commission, *Height and Weight Requirements in Employment*

4 New Brunswick Human Rights Commission, *Employment Application Forms and other Pre-employment Inquiries*; Ontario Human Rights Commission, *Policy on Hiring;* see below, Chapter 4. Medical Issues and Chapter 7 Accommodating Substance Abuse

5 *Canada (Attorney General) v. Girouard*, 2002 CarswellNat 1195, 2002 CarswellNat 1664, 2002 FCA 224, 2002 CAF 224, 2002 C.L.L.C. 210-028, 291 N.R. 289, [2002] 4 F.C. 538, 226 F.T.R. 223 (note) (Fed. C.A.); *Tremblay v. Canada (Attorney General)*, 2003 CarswellNat 1048, 2003 CarswellNat 2695, 2003 FCT 466, 2003 CFPI 466 (Fed. T.D.); *Green v. Canada (Public Service Commission)*, 2000 CarswellNat 1110, 2000 C.L.L.C. 230-024, 2000 CarswellNat 3278, 1 C.C.E.L. (3d) 1, [2000] 4 F.C. 629, 183 F.T.R. 161, 38 C.H.R.R. D/1 (Fed. T.D.); *Justice Institute of British Columbia v. British Columbia (Attorney General)* (1999), 1999 CarswellBC 1481, 17 Admin. L.R. (3d) 267, 99 C.L.L.C. 230-023 (B.C. S.C.)

6 Ontario Human Rights Commission, *Employment-Related Medical Information*

7 *Bonner v. Ontario (Minister of Health)* (1992), 16 C.H.R.R. D/485, 92 C.L.L.C. 17,019 (Ont. Bd. of Inquiry)

8 Appendix B: Alberta Human Rights Commission, *Duty to Accommodate;* Ontario Human Rights Commission, *Disability and the Duty to Accommodate*; see also B.C. Human Rights Commission, *The Duty to Accommodate*; see below, Chapter 4 Medical Issues

9 *Parisien v. Ottawa-Carlton Transit Comm.*, 2003 CHRT 10 (Can. Human Rights Trib.); *Cache Creek (Village) v. I.U.O.E., Local 115C*

(2002), 2002 CarswellBC 2482, 105 L.A.C. (4th) 97 (B.C. Arb. Bd.); *Sylvester v. British Columbia Society of Male Survivors of Sexual Abuse*, 2002 CarswellBC 3216, 2003 C.L.L.C. 230-004, 2002 BCHRT 14, 43 C.H.R.R. D/55 (B.C. Human Rights Trib.); *Mainland Sawmills v. IWA-Canada, Local 2171* (2002), 2002 CarswellBC 2465, 104 L.A.C. (4th) 385 (B.C. Arb. Bd.); *Grober Inc. v. U.F.C.W., Local 175* (2002), 2002 CarswellOnt 4763, 109 L.A.C. (4th) 53 (Ont. Arb. Bd.); Ottawa Civic Hospital v. O.N.A. (1995), 1995 CarswellOnt 1438, 48 L.A.C. (4th) 388 (Ont. Arb. Bd.); Galt & Harding. "No safety in the numbers." *Globe and Mail* June 18, 2003; Appendix B, Ontario Human Rights Commission, *Disability and the Duty to Accommodate*

[10] *Chambly (Commission scolaire régionale) v. Bergevin*, 21 Admin. L.R. (2d) 169, 1994 CarswellQue 78, 1994 CarswellQue 114, 4 C.C.E.L. (2d) 165, 169 N.R. 281, 94 C.L.L.C. 17,023, 62 Q.A.C. 241, [1994] 2 S.C.R. 525, 115 D.L.R. (4th) 609, 22 C.H.R.R. D/1 (S.C.C.); *Renaud v. Central Okanagan School District No. 23*, [1992] 2 S.C.R. 970, 1992 CarswellBC 257, 1992 CarswellBC 910, [1992] 6 W.W.R. 193, 95 D.L.R. (4th) 577, 24 W.A.C. 245, 92 C.L.L.C. 17,032, 141 N.R. 185, 71 B.C.L.R. (2d) 145, 13 B.C.A.C. 245, 16 C.H.R.R. D/425 (S.C.C.); *C.L.C., Local 102 v. Dearness Home* (2001), 2001 CarswellOnt 4934, [2002] L.V.I. 3266-6 (Ont. Arb. Bd.); *Bubb-Clarke v. Toronto Transit Commission* (2002), 2002 CarswellOnt 3764, 2002 C.L.L.C. 230-032, 42 C.H.R.R. D/326 (Ont. Bd. of Inquiry); *N.S.G.E.U. v. Nova Scotia (Human Resources)*, 1999 CarswellNS 173, [1999] L.V.I. 3012-1 (N.S. Arb. Bd.); *West Park Hospital v. O.N.A.*, 1996 CarswellOnt 5356, 55 L.A.C. (4th) 78, [1996] L.V.I. 2756-3 (Ont. Arb. Bd.)

[11] *Unilever HPC NA v. Teamsters, Chemical, Energy & Allied Workers, Local 132* (2002), 2002 CarswellOnt 4749, 106 L.A.C. (4th) 360 (Ont. Arb. Bd.). But see *Brampton (City) v. A.T.U., Local 1573* (1998), 1998 CarswellOnt 5660, 75 L.A.C. (4th) 163 (Ont. Arb. Bd.) which indicated the employee has to prove the ability to perform other duties the employer may reasonably have available.

[12] For tribunal and court decisions on these issues, see below, Chapter 4 Medical Issues and Chapter 5 Suitable Alternative Employment.

[13] *West Park Hospital v. O.N.A.*, 1996 CarswellOnt 5356, 55 L.A.C. (4th) 78, [1996] L.V.I. 2756-3 (Ont. Arb. Bd.)

[14] *Hutchinson v. Canada (Minister of Environment)*, 2003 CarswellNat 679, 2003 FCA 133, 302 N.R. 66, 25 C.C.E.L. (3d) 206, 50 Admin.

L.R. (3d) 255 (Fed. C.A.); *Ontario (Ministry of Community & Social Services) v. O.P.S.E.U.* (2000), 50 O.R. (3d) 560, 2000 CarswellOnt 3183, 2 C.C.E.L. (3d) 302, 191 D.L.R. (4th) 489, 136 O.A.C. 35, 2001 C.L.L.C. 230-010 (Ont. C.A.)

[15] *Renaud v. Central Okanagan School District No. 23*, [1992] 2 S.C.R. 970, 1992 CarswellBC 257, 1992 CarswellBC 910, [1992] 6 W.W.R. 193, 95 D.L.R. (4th) 577, 24 W.A.C. 245, 92 C.L.L.C. 17,032, 141 N.R. 185, 71 B.C.L.R. (2d) 145, 13 B.C.A.C. 245, 16 C.H.R.R. D/425 (S.C.C.); Lynk, S. "Accommodation, Disability and the Unionized Canadian Workplace." *Human Rights in the Unionized Workplace*, C.B.A.O., Continuing Legal Education: 2001.

[16] *N.S.G.E.U. v. Nova Scotia (Human Resources)*, 1999 CarswellNS 173, [1999] L.V.I. 3012-1 (N.S. Arb. Bd.); *Waterloo Furniture Components v. U.S.W.A., Local 7155* (1999), [2000] L.V.I. 3076-5, 1999 CarswellOnt 4618 (Ont. Arb. Bd.); Appendix B: Alberta Human Rights Commission, *The Duty to Accommodate* and see below, Chapter 4 Medical Issues

◆

CHAPTER 4

MEDICAL ISSUES

- Pre-employment Medical Exams and Testing
- Disclosure of Diagnosis and Treatment
- Medical Opinions
- Summary

How much medical information must a disabled employee disclose? And when should this be disclosed? The employee is concerned about privacy and what will happen to the medical information disclosed; there may be a tendency to reveal as little as possible. On the other hand, the employer may attempt to find out every detail related to the disability, wanting to be assured that its employees are capable of safely fulfilling all the essential job duties.

Pre-Employment Medical Exams and Testing

Some employers have tried to use medical tests and exams as part of the selection process. According to human rights law, before a formal (written) offer of employment, medical exams are not permissible. Nor is HIV/AIDS testing acceptable.[1] After a formal offer of employment, medical exams may be permissible. Their purpose must be solely to determine whether the applicant can perform the essential duties of the job. HIV/AIDS testing would only rarely be related to the essential duties of a job and therefore is rarely acceptable.[2]

Disclosure of Diagnosis and Treatment

On the job, when an employee asks for accommodation of a disability, an employer cannot rely on impressionistic, speculative evidence of the work the employee is capable of doing.[3] This puts the onus on the employee to make available all relevant information within their control to define what their needs are.[4] At the same time, the employee's duty to provide medical information must be consistent with their privacy rights.[5] So the employer must rely on medical advice. But what is the scope of that advice? And who should provide it?

Generally, human rights commissions have advised that disabled employees should set out their functional limitations and needs, not the nature of their medical condition, not the diagnosis; for this, their doctor's certificate is sufficient.[6] However, tribunals have gone beyond that, indicating that the employee must provide not only the prognosis, but also the diagnosis and prove the connection between the inability to perform the essential duties of the job and the disability. Where the employer contests the existence of a disability, this information is particularly important. In most cases, the employee will have to produce medical evidence sufficient to allow the employer to match the abilities of the employee to the demands of a job. Never should an employee be expected to provide medical information unrelated to the disability to be accommodated.[7]

Medical Opinions

In some situations, the employer may require the employee to undergo a medical examination by a doctor of the employer's choice or by a specialist. Or it may have to consult a specialist in terms of whether a particular disability, in general, has a negative impact on a person's capacity to perform the essential duties of a job. However, if an employer has doubts regarding the report provided by an employee's doctor, it cannot reject the advice without first speaking with the doctor.[8]

According to the Ontario Human Rights Commission, employers should bear the cost of any required medical information, paying for medical opinions and letters setting out accommodation needs. Also, it is best to leave medical information with the examining physician and to keep it away from the disabled employee's supervisor, out of the personnel file.[9]

Summary

The issue of medical information can be extremely contentious. A disabled employee is often under tremendous pressure when making a request for accommodation, mentally, physically and financially; moreover, they want to maintain their privacy. From the employer's point of view, a request for accommodation may be a surprise, it may be questionable or it may be extremely disruptive.

The privacy rights of both the job applicant and the employee are protected. Medical exams and testing are permissible in circumscribed circumstances and initially, at least, the employee need not reveal the diagnosis and treatment. The issue is the functional limitations and needs of the employee seeking accommodation, and for this a family doctor's certificate is usually sufficient, but not always. The employer must have information sufficient to permit it to match the employee's abilities with job duties.

ENDNOTES

[1] Canadian Human Rights Comission, *Policy on HIV/AIDS*; New Brunswick Human Rights Commission, *Employment Application Forms and other Pre-employment Inquiries*; Ontario Human Rights Commission, *Employment-Related Medical Information*

[2] Canadian Human Rights Comission, *Policy on HIV/AIDS*; New Brunswick Human Rights Commission, *Employment Application Forms and other Pre-employment Inquiries* and *General Criteria for the Investigation of Complaints of HIV/AIDS Discrimination*; Ontario Human Rights Commission, *Employment-Related Medical Information*; see below, Chapter 7 Reasonable Accommodation and Substance Abuse

[3] *Municipal Assn. of Police Personnel v. Halifax (Regional Municipality)* (2002), 2002 CarswellNS 555, 105 L.A.C. (4th) 232 (N.S. Arb. Bd.); *Jeppesen v. Ancaster (Town) Fire & Emergency Services* (2001), 2001 C.L.L.C. 230-013, 2001 CarswellOnt 5333, 39 C.H.R.R. D/177 (Ont. Bd. of Inquiry); *Cameron v. Nel-Gor Castle Nursing Home* (1984), 5 C.H.R.R. D/2170, 84 C.L.L.C. 17,008 (Ont. Bd. of Inquiry), leave to appeal refused (November 25, 1985), No. 456/84 (Ont. Div. Ct.)

[4] *Reimer v. York (Regional Police)* (October 6, 1998), No. 98-017 (Ont. Bd. of Inquiry); *Thermal Ceramics v. U.S.W.A.* (1992), 30 L.A.C. (4th) 314, 1992 CarswellOnt 1274 (Ont. Arb. Bd.)

[5] *Ontario (Human Rights Commission) v. Dofasco Inc.* (2001), 2001 CarswellOnt 4049, 151 O.A.C. 201, 208 D.L.R. (4th) 276, 14 C.C.E.L.

(3d) 165, 57 O.R. (3d) 693, 39 Admin. L.R. (3d) 199, 41 C.H.R.R. D/237 (Ont. C.A.)

[6] See Appendix B, Alberta Human Rights Commission, *Duty Accommodate*; Ontario Human Rights Commission, *Disability and the Duty to* Accommodate; see also B.C. Human Rights Commission, *The Duty to Accommodate*

[7] *Kodak Canada Inc. v. Employees' Assn. of Kodak Canada* (2002), 2002 CarswellOnt 5389, 113 L.A.C. (4th) 416 (Ont. Arb. Bd.); *Toronto Teachers' Federation v. Toronto (City) Board of Education*, 1997 CarswellOnt 3855, [1997] L.V.I. 2864-5 (Ont. Arb. Bd.); *Municipal Assn. of Police Personnel v. Halifax (Regional Municipality)* (2002), 2002 CarswellNS 555, 105 L.A.C. (4th) 232 (N.S. Arb. Bd.); *Pacholko v. Patel* (2001), 2001 CarswellSask 859, 2002 C.L.L.C. 230-004 (Sask. Bd. of Inquiry); *Brampton (City) v. A.T.U., Local 1573* (1998), 1998 CarswellOnt 5660, 75 L.A.C. (4th) 163 (Ont. Arb. Bd.); *Dominion Castings Ltd. v. U.S.W.A., Local 9392* (1998), 1998 CarswellOnt 5515, 73 L.A.C. (4th) 347 (Ont. Arb. Bd.); *Reimer v. York (Regional Police)* (October 6, 1998), No. 98-017 (Ont. Bd. of Inquiry); *Toronto Teachers' Federation v. Toronto (City) Board of Education*, 1997 CarswellOnt 3855, [1997] L.V.I. 2864-5 (Ont. Arb. Bd.)

[8] *Ontario (Human Rights Commission) v. Dofasco Inc.* (2001), 2001 CarswellOnt 4049, 151 O.A.C. 201, 208 D.L.R. (4th) 276, 14 C.C.E.L. (3d) 165, 57 O.R. (3d) 693, 39 Admin. L.R. (3d) 199, 41 C.H.R.R. D/237 (Ont. C.A.); *Kodak Canada Inc. v. Employees' Assn. of Kodak Canada* (2002), 2002 CarswellOnt 5389, 113 L.A.C. (4th) 416 (Ont. Arb. Bd.); *Bubb-Clarke v. Toronto Transit Commission* (2002), 2002 CarswellOnt 3764, 2002 C.L.L.C. 230-032, 42 C.H.R.R. D/326 (Ont. Bd. of Inquiry); *Toronto Teachers' Federation v. Toronto (City) Board of Education* (1997), 1997 CarswellOnt 3855, [1977] L.V.I. 2864-5 (Ont. Arb. Bd.); *Chamberlin v. 599273 Ontario Ltd.* (1989), 11 C.H.R.R. D/110 (Ont. Bd. of Inquiry); Appendix B: Alberta Human Rights Commission, *The Duty to Accommodate*; Ontario Human Rights Commission, *Disability and the Duty to Accommodate*; and see below Chapter 7 Reasonable Accommodation and Substance Abuse

[9] See Appendix B, Ontario Rights Commission, *Disability and the Duty to Accommodate*

◆

CHAPTER 5

SUITABLE ALTERNATIVE EMPLOYMENT

- Return to Work
- Part-Time Work
- Temporary Reassignment
- Assumption of Risk
- Training
- Seniority
- Collective Agreement
- Wages and Benefits
- Efficiency
- Summary

One of the possibilities considered in accommodating a disability is whether suitable alternative employment is available. In investigating this issue, the employer is expected to broaden the scope very wide. This may include creating a new position with rebundled tasks, depending on the nature and size of the business, cost, interests of co-workers, health and safety, contracts (including the collective agreement) and disruption of operations.[1] The bottom line is that the alternate work must assist the employer to provide its service or product in an efficient and economical manner.

Return to Work

There are two lines of thinking with respect to how far the employer must go in creating work for a disabled employee. The older view is that the employer only has to assess whether a disabled employee is capable of performing the essential duties of his/her position or an available position. More recently, tribunals have found that the employer should modify an existing position or even create a new position by putting together a bundle of tasks within the employee's limitations.[2]

Part-Time Work

In any event, where possible, the employer should permit a gradual return to work and should not require a disabled employee to be completely recovered and able to perform full time work.[3]

Temporary Reassignment

The disabled employee may be assigned to a new position on a temporary basis. The expected duration of this type of accommodation is only one factor to be taken into account. Even if a maximum time limit is necessary to avoid undue hardship, this limit should be fixed on the basis of concrete facts, not impressionistic evidence or by the exercise of unfettered managerial discretion.[4]

Assumption of Risk

With respect to safety, the employer should not set standards that are higher than necessary, irrelevant to the task performed or exclusionary with respect to some classes of people on the basis of disability. The evidence of risk must be objective, not impressionistic, and employees should be allowed to make their own reasonably informed employment and medical choices.[5]

Overall, the employer must take suitable precautions to reduce risk; this is part of the duty to accommodate. While risk is considered in the analysis of hardship to the employer, it cannot be an independent justification for discrimination.[6] The Ontario Human Rights Commission has addressed this issue in detail in *Disability and the Duty to Accommodate*.[7] In its view, a disabled employee may, in some circumstances, assume a risk and ask the employer to modify or waive a health and safety requirement. However, if the risk of harm to the disabled employee is significant, probable and serious, this is not acceptable.

To assess the seriousness of the risk, it is necessary to address the nature of the potential harm and the probability it will occur. Thus, if the harm caused would be minor and is not likely to occur, the risk would not be considered serious. This assessment must be conducted in the context of recognizing the risks inherent in the nature of the business or industry and other sources of risk, such as employee fatigue.

A similar analysis relating to harm to others, that is, co-workers and the public, would also be necessary. Where the risk is solely to the disabled employee, the degree of acceptable risk is higher than where the risk is to others. In all cases, the employer must inform those affected of the risk.

Training

Training may be required in the course of accommodation.[8] However, there are limits to this and sometimes disabled employees may have to acquire training using their own resources or workers' compensation programs.[9]

Seniority

In the past, arbitrators have found that a new position should be the most preferable of the jobs available, in accordance with seniority.[10] Earlier decisions of tribunals in three provinces found that the duty to accommodate in a unionized workplace does not require an employer to displace an employee or an incumbent and give the position to a disabled employee.[11] Recently, however, tribunals have indicated that seniority provisions in collective agreements are less determinative.[12]

At the same time, employers must develop options with the union. They cannot merely suspend seniority provisions, suspend job posting provisions and award a new position directly to a disabled employee.[13] Nor can unions and employers sign a collective agreement which prevents a union member from maintaining the same seniority level upon transfer from one division to another; this provision discriminates against employees who need to change divisions to accommodate a disability.[14]

Collective Agreement

Generally, the duty to accommodate prevails over contracts, such as collective agreements. However, a substantial departure from the normal operation of the collective agreement may amount to undue interference in the operation of the business and may constitute undue hardship to the employer.[15]

In a unionized environment, the employer must make an effort to accommodate the disability in a position within the bargaining unit. If accommodation is only possible in a position excluded from the bargaining unit, the disabled employee should retain rights with respect to seniority, service and benefits. Moreover, both the employer and the union are under a continuing duty to facilitate the return of the disabled employee to the bargaining unit as part of the duty to accommodate. However, full bargaining unit status and the continuation of union dues do not form part of the accommodation.[16]

For its part, the union has a duty to represent the best interests of all its members, not just the disabled union member. Thus, if an employer proposes an accommodation which would disrupt the collective agreement or otherwise negatively affect the interests of co-workers, the union could withhold its agreement. Overall, options to accommodate must balance the interests of the employer and those of all union members, as expressed in the collective agreement. If the union objects to accommodation proposed by the employer, it may be required to propose alternative measures which reflect the provisions of the collective agreement. However, if the most sensible option requires a change to the collective agreement, the union must work with the employer to make that change.[17]

Wages and Benefits

Ideally, the accommodation will be comparable to the old job in terms of hours, remuneration and benefits.[18] When the only available position a disabled employee can perform with modification is a lower-rated position, the employee should be paid at the lower rate.[19] Moreover, an employee who transfers from full-time to part-time hours after recovery from a disability is not entitled to the same benefit coverage as a full-time employee; the benefits should be based on the number of hours worked.[20]

Efficiency

Human rights law does not require employers to hire or retain employees who, because of a disability, are incapable of doing the work, simply because the employer has the resources to tolerate deficient work performance.[21] Nor is the employer required to create a position which does not assist it in getting the work done in an efficient and economical manner. It would be undue hardship for the employer to create an unnecessary position.[22]

Moreover, where a disabled employee is unable to perform a particular task and this constitutes the major part of the job, it is not acceptable for co-workers to assist with these duties. Nor should the employer have to hire an additional employee to assist with these duties.[23]

Summary

In considering what alternate employment might be available, there are several options to consider. These range from reducing the duties of the old job to those that are essential to creating a new position with rebundled tasks. This job might be full-time or part-time, temporary or permanent and might involve retraining. But any return to work should assist the employer in an efficient and economical manner and should be remunerated according to the tasks performed and the hours worked. The collective agreement must be taken into account, as must seniority; however, neither are determinative.

ENDNOTES

[1]   See above, Chapter 1 Reasonable Accommodation and Undue Hardship

[2]   *Beznochuk v. Spruceland Terminals Ltd.* (1996), 1996 CarswellBC 2828, 32 B.C.L.R. (3d) 7, 84 B.C.A.C. 230, 137 W.A.C. 230, 97 C.L.L.C. 230-026, 29 C.H.R.R. D/269 (B.C. C.A.); *Biltrite Industries v. U.S.W.A.* (2002), 2002 CarswellOnt 5255, 112 L.A.C. (4th) 385 (Ont. Arb. Bd.); *Essex Police Services Board v. Essex Police Assn.* (2002), 2002 CarswellOnt 3455, 105 L.A.C. (4th) 193 (Ont. Police Arb. Comm.); *C.L.C., Local 102 v. Dearness Home* (2001), 2001 CarswellOnt 4934, [2002] L.V.I. 3266-6 (Ont. Arb. Bd.); *O.P.S.E.U. v. Hotel Dieu Hospital*, 2001 CarswellOnt 4735, [2001] L.V.I. 3240-6 (Ont. Arb. Bd.); *Metsala v. Falconbridge Ltd.* (2001), 2001 C.L.L.C. 230-029, [2001] O.H.R.B.I.D. No. 5, 2001 CarswellOnt 5743, 39 C.H.R.R. D/153 (Ont. Bd. of Inquiry); *Hamilton (City) Hydro-Electric Commission v. I.B.E.W., Local 138* (1997), 1997 CarswellOnt 1533 (Ont. Arb. Bd.); *O.P.S.E.U. v. O.E.C.T.A.* (1996), 1996 CarswellOnt 5446, [1997] L.V.I. 2842-5 (Ont. Arb. Bd.); *U.F.C.W., Locals 175 & 633 v. Community Nursing Home — Port Hope*, 1996 CarswellOnt

5429, [1996] L.V.I. 2809-7 (Ont. Arb. Bd.); *Calgary District Hospital Group v. U.N.A., Local 121-R*, 41 L.A.C. (4th) 319, 1994 CarswellAlta 773, [1994] L.V.I. 2618-5 (Alta. Arb. Bd.); *York County Hospital v. O.N.A.* (1992), 26 L.A.C. (4th) 384, 1992 CarswellOnt 1201 (Ont. Arb. Bd.); Lynk, S., "Accommodation, Disability and the Unionized Workplace" in *Human Rights in the Unionized* Workplace, C.BA.O., Continiuing Legal Education: 2001; Appendix B: Ontario Human Rights Commission, *Disability and the Duty to Accommodate;* see also B.C. Human Rights Commission, *The Duty to Accommodate*

[3] *Skopitz v. Intercorp Excelle Foods Inc.* (1999), 1999 CarswellOnt 2050, [1999] O.J. No. 1543, 43 C.C.E.L. (2d) 253 (Ont. Gen. Div.); *Shirley v. Eecol Electric (Sask.) Ltd.* (2001), 2001 CarswellSask 255, 2001 C.L.L.C. 230-021, 39 C.H.R.R. D/168 (Sask. Bd. of Inquiry); *Marzano v. Nathar Ltd.* (1992), 18 C.H.R.R. D/248 (Ont. Bd. of Inquiry)

[4] *Municipal Assn. of Police Personnel v. Halifax (Regional Municipality)* (2002), 2002 CarswellNS 555, 105 L.A.C. (4th) 232 (N.S. Arb. Bd.)

[5] *British Columbia (Public Service Employee Relations Commission) v. B.C.G.E.U.*, [1999] 3 S.C.R. 3, 1999 CarswellBC 1907, 1999 CarswellBC 1908, [1999] S.C.J. No. 46, 99 C.L.L.C. 230-028, [1999] 10 W.W.R. 1, 176 D.L.R. (4th) 1, 244 N.R. 145, 66 B.C.L.R. (3d) 253, 127 B.C.A.C. 161, 207 W.A.C. 161, 46 C.C.E.L. (2d) 206, 35 C.H.R.R. D/257, 68 C.R.R. (2d) 1, 7 B.H.R.C. 437 (S.C.C.); *Heincke v. Brownell* (1992), 55 O.A.C. 33, 1992 CarswellOnt 905, 92 C.L.L.C. 17,012, 90 D.L.R. (4th) 476, 4 Admin. L.R. (2d) 212, 41 C.C.E.L. 307, 16 C.H.R.R. D/300 (Ont. Div. Ct.); *O.P.S.E.U. v. Hotel Dieu Hospital*, 2001 CarswellOnt 4735, [2001] L.V.I. 3240-6 (Ont. Arb. Bd.)

[6] B.C. Human Rights Commission, *The Duty to Accommodate*

[7] See Appendix B

[8] *York County Hospital v. O.N.A.* (1992), 26 L.A.C. (4th) 384, 1992 CarswellOnt 1201 (Ont. Arb. Bd.)

[9] *Biltrite Industries v. U.S.W.A.* (2002), 2002 CarswellOnt 5255, 112 L.A.C. (4th) 385 (Ont. Arb. Bd.); Lynk, S., "Accommodation, Disability and the Unionized Workplace", in *Human Rights in the Unionized* Workplace, C.B.A.O., Continiuing Legal Education: 2001

[10] *Thunder Bay (City) v. S.E.I.U., Local, 268* (1992), 27 L.A.C. (4th) 194, 1992 CarswellOnt 1210 (Ont. Arb. Bd.)

[11] *Beznochuk v. Spruceland Terminals Ltd.* (1999), 1999 CarswellBC 3116, [1999] B.C.H.R.T.D. No. 45, 2000 C.L.L.C. 230-004, 37 C.H.R.R. D/259 (B.C. Human Rights Trib.); *N.S.G.E.U. v. Nova Scotia (Human Resources)* 1999 CarswellNS 173 (N.S. Arb. Bd.); *Hamilton (City) Hydro-Electric Commission v. I.B.E.W., Local 138* (1997), 1997 CarswellOnt 1533 (Ont. Arb. Bd.)

[12] *Welland County General Hospital v. S.E.I.U., Local 204,* [2000] L.V.I. 3104-1, 2000 CarswellOnt 1901 (Ont. Arb. Bd.). For instance, in a 2001 decision, an Ontario arbitrator indicated the employer might have to give a job to a handicapped employee in preference to more senior applicants. (*C.L.C., Local 102 v. Dearness Home* (2001), 2001 CarswellOnt 4934, [2002] L.V.I. 3266-6 (Ont. Arb. Bd.)). Clearly, where both employees are disabled, seniority is the defining factor. *Babcock & Wilcox Canada v. U.S.W.A., Local 2859,* 2003 CarswellOnt 1860, [2003] L.V.I. 3359-1 (Ont. Arb. Bd.)

[13] *Welland County General Hospital v. S.E.I.U., Local 204,* [2000] L.V.I. 3104-1, 2000 CarswellOnt 1901 (Ont. Arb. Bd.)

[14] *Bubb-Clarke v. Toronto Transit Commission* (2002), 2002 CarswellOnt 3764, 2002 C.L.L.C. 230-032, 42 C.H.R.R. D/326 (Ont. Bd. of Inquiry). But see B.C. Human Rights Commission, *The Duty to Accommodate*

[15] B.C. Human Rights Commission, *The Duty to Accommodate*

[16] *C.L.C., Local 102 v. Dearness Home* (2001), 2001 CarswellOnt 4934, [2002] L.V.I. 3266-6 (Ont. Arb. Bd.); *West Park Hospital v. O.N.A.,* 1996 CarswellOnt 5356, 55 L.A.C. (4th) 78, [1996] L.V.I. 2756-3 (Ont. Arb. Bd.). But see B.C. Human Rights Commission, *The Duty to Accommodate.*

[17] B.C. Human Rights Commission, *The Duty to Accommodate*

[18] *York County Hospital v. O.N.A.* (1992), 26 L.A.C. (4th) 384, 1992 CarswellOnt 1201 (Ont. Arb. Bd.)

[19] *O.P.S.E.U. v. O.E.C.T.A.* (1996), 1996 CarswellOnt 5446, [1997] L.V.I. 2842-5 (Ont. Arb. Bd.); *Fenwick Automotive v. U.S.W.A.,* 84 L.A.C. (4th) 271, 1999 CarswellOnt 4428, [1999] O.L.A.A. No. 702, [1999] L.V.I. 3062-4 (Ont. Arb. Bd.)

[20] *O.N.A. v. Orillia Soldiers Memorial Hospital* (1999), 42 O.R. (3d) 692, 1999 CarswellOnt 28, [1999] O.J. No. 44, 40 C.C.E.L. (2d) 263, 99 C.L.L.C. 230-007, 169 D.L.R. (4th) 489, 117 O.A.C. 146, 20 C.C.P.B. 195, 36 C.H.R.R. D/202 (Ont. C.A.), leave to appeal refused (1999), 252 N.R. 196 (note), [1999] S.C.C.A. No. 118, 133 O.A.C.

199 (note) (S.C.C.); *Crossroads Regional Health Authority v. A.U.P.E.* (2002), 2002 CarswellAlta 1223, 105 L.A.C. (4th) 78 (Alta. Arb. Bd.); *Cambridge Memorial Hospital v. O.N.A.* (1999), 79 L.A.C. (4th) 392, 1999 CarswellOnt 3231 (Ont. Arb. Bd.); *Messier-Dowty Inc. v. I.A.M.A.W., Local 905* (1999), 80 L.A.C. (4th) 87, 1999 CarswellOnt 3616 (Ont. Arb. Bd.). See also Chapter 6 Absence from Work — Benefits.

[21] *Bonner v. Ontario (Minister of Health)* (1992), 16 C.H.R.R. D/485, 92 C.L.L.C. 17,019 (Ont. Bd. of Inquiry)

[22] *Essex Police Services Board v. Essex Police Assn.* (2002), 2002 CarswellOnt 3455, 105 L.A.C. (4th) 193 (Ont. Police Arb. Comm.); *U.S.W.A., Local 9042 v. Iko Industries Ltd.*, 2001 CarswellOnt 5116, [2001] L.V.I. 3298-3 (Ont. Arb. Bd.); *Wilfrid Laurier University v. U.F.C.W., Local 175*, 2000 CarswellOnt 2492, [2000] L.V.I. 3113-2 (Ont. Arb. Bd.); *International Union of Elevator Constructors, Local 96 v. Otis Canada Inc.* (August 14, 1999), Doc. 3170-95-G (Ont. Arb. Bd.); *N.S.G.E.U. v. Nova Scotia (Human Resources)*, 1999 CarswellNS 173, [1999] L.V.I. 3012-1 (N.S. Arb. Bd.)

[23] *U.F.C.W., Locals 175 & 633 v. Community Nursing Home — Port Hope*, 1996 CarswellOnt 5429, [1996] L.V.I. 2809-7 (Ont. Arb. Bd.); *Marzano v. Nathar Ltd.* (1992), 18 C.H.R.R. D/248 (Ont. Bd. of Inquiry)

♦

CHAPTER 6

ABSENCE FROM WORK

- Benefits
  - Monetary
  - Non-monetary
- Length of Absence
  - Long-term
  - Intermittent
- Last Chance Agreements
- Status under the Collective Agreement
- Temporary Replacement
- Summary

Ordinarily, the employer is required to permit an employee's absence to recover from a disability and should have administrative procedures in place to provide this form of accommodation, where it would not cause undue hardship. Depending on the nature and severity of a disability, absences from work may be planned or unplanned. They may also be short, long-term or intermittent. However, the employer's duty to accommodate employee absences is not determined by the nature of the absence.[1]

There is no fixed rule defining the length of an acceptable absence under human rights legislation. This depends on many factors, unique to each case, such as: the workplace circumstances, the employee's prognosis and the length, predictability and frequency of the absences. A policy which relies on arbitrarily selected cut-offs or that requires an inflexible date of return may be challenged as a breach of human rights legislation.[2]

Benefits

What should be done about employee benefits during a disability leave? Employee benefits are treated differently in human rights law, depending on whether they are monetary or non-monetary. Monetary benefits are those which constitute a form of compensation for work, such as: vacation pay, sick benefits and bonuses. All other types of benefits are defined as non-monetary.

Monetary

Monetary benefits for disabled employees who are unable to work should not be the same as those received by employees providing work. This is the case unless the collective agreement indicates otherwise.[3] However, the monetary benefits paid to disabled employees while on disability leave should be the same and an employer must take care to treat all types of disability in the same manner. No distinction should be made on the basis of type of disability, whether in the quantum of benefits paid or the length of disability leave.[4]

Non-Monetary

There are many non-monetary benefits which should not be affected by a disability leave; for instance, seniority accrual, determination of vacation benefits, re-call rights and the opportunity to apply for closed job competitions.[5] These benefits are not compensation for work and must be the same for all employees, whether actively employed or on leave.[6]

Nature of Absence

Long-term

Where an absence is long-term, and temporary replacement of the disabled employee is possible, the parties should ensure open communication to assess developments as time goes by. Because the employer has the primary duty to identify possible accommodation, it should ensure that it makes an assessment of the circumstances. At some point, it may not be possible to keep the position open or give a rehiring preference to the disabled employee.[7]

How long an employer must maintain the employment status of an absent disabled employee depends, first of all, on the prognosis for a return to work. If medical reports indicate there is a reasonable prospect of a return to work in the foreseeable future, the employer must try to hold off. The second issue is whether there has been excessive absenteeism. The employer may have to wait eighteen months to discharge a disabled employee, depending, among other factors, on what is considered excessive absenteeism in that particular workplace[8] and whether the absence has created difficulties for the employer and/or co-workers.[9] The employer does not have to accommodate employee absences indefinitely where there is no prospect that the employee's disability will improve.[10]

Intermittent

With regard to intermittent and unpredictable absenteeism, there are several relevant factors: the number and regularity of absences, availability of substitute employees and prognosis for regular attendance.[11] In some cases, the most reliable predictor of future attendance is the disabled employee's long-term attendance history.[12] The assessment of undue hardship must be based on every accommodative measure taken throughout the period of the handicap. This should include the burden of all absences caused by the disability, including those which occur both before and after the employee informs the employer of the disability.[13]

Last Chance Agreements

Some employers have attempted to deal with employee absences due to disability through the use of last chance agreements. But, except in Alberta, last chance agreements relating to handicap are subject to the duty to accommodate.[14] Moreover, an employer cannot necessarily require a disabled employee to maintain a certain attendance level following past absenteeism due to handicap. Like all work rules or standards, this is subject to the duty to accommodate.[15]

Status under the Collective Agreement

A disabled employee maintains full-time permanent status under the union contract during an absence from work for convalescence. For this reason, the employee's absence from work during an update of technological training does not create a disqualification in terms of the training upon return to work.[16]

Temporary Replacement

How should the absent employee's work tasks be completed? The employer may have to employ a temporary replacement while the disabled employee is absent from the workplace during recovery.[17] In some circumstances, however, the employer cannot provide a temporary replacement without undue hardship. This may be due to the length of the absence, the size of the business or the size of the department in which the disabled employee works.

Summary

Where a disabled employee needs to take time away from work, ordinarily, the employer is required to permit the absence and should have administrative procedures in place for this purpose. There is no fixed rule defining the length of an acceptable absence under human rights legislation. This depends on many factors, unique to each case, particularly the prognosis for return to work. With respect to intermittent absences, last chance agreements can be useful to set out expectations; however, these agreements are subject to the duty to accommodate.

When an employee is on disability leave, the employer must address the payment of benefits and decide how the absent employee's work will be performed during the absence. Monetary benefits for absent disabled employees should not be the same as those for employees who are working. However, there should be no distinction with respect to non-monetary benefits

Depending on the length of absence, it may be possible for an employer to keep the absent employee's position open for a period of time. To deal with this, the employer may hire a temporary employee or divide the absent employee's work duties among other employees. If this is not possible, the employer may have to find a permanent replacement.

ENDNOTES

[1] *Chamberlin v. 599273 Ontario Ltd.* (1989), 11 C.H.R.R. D/110 (Ont. Bd. of Inquiry)

[2] *Sylvester v. British Columbia Society of Male Survivors of Sexual Abuse,* 2002 CarswellBC 3216, 2003 C.L.L.C. 230-004, 2002 BCHRT 14, 43 C.H.R.R. D/55 (B.C. Human Rights Trib.); Appendix B, Ontario Human Rights Commission, *Disability and the Duty to Accommodate).* For instance, a policy permitting dismissal of employees who request sick leave in excess of five days per year is discriminatory. (*Bielecky v. Young, MacNamara* (1992), 20 C.H.R.R. D/215 (Ont. Bd. of Inquiry) and see below, Chapter 8 Discharge

[3] *O.N.A. v. Orillia Soldiers Memorial Hospital* (1999), 42 O.R. (3d) 692, 1999 CarswellOnt 28, [1999] O.J. No. 44, 40 C.C.E.L. (2d) 263, 99 C.L.L.C. 230-007, 169 D.L.R. (4th) 489, 117 O.A.C. 146, 20 C.C.P.B. 195, 36 C.H.R.R. D/202 (Ont. C.A.), leave to appeal refused (1999), 252 N.R. 196 (note), [1999] S.C.C.A. No. 118, 133 O.A.C. 199 (note) (S.C.C.); *Real Canadian Superstore v. U.F.C.W., Local 1400,* 2000 CarswellSask 356, [2000] S.J. No. 334, 2000 SKCA 64, 187 D.L.R. (4th) 759, [2000] 7 W.W.R. 579, 199 Sask. R. 18, 232 W.A.C. 18 (Sask. C.A.), leave to appeal refused (2001), 2001 CarswellSask 28, 2001 CarswellSask 29, [2000] S.C.C.A. No. 377, 267 N.R. 198 (note), 219 Sask. R. 320 (note), 272 W.A.C. 320 (note) (S.C.C.), leave to appeal refused (2001), 2001 CarswellSask 30, 2001 CarswellSask 31, [2000] S.C.C.A. No. 378, 267 N.R. 199 (note), 213 Sask. R. 320 (note), 260 W.A.C. 320 (note) (S.C.C.); *Canada (Human Rights Commission) v. Canadian National Railway (Terra Transport)* (2000), 2000 CarswellNat 1223, 2000 C.L.L.C. 230-036, 192 F.T.R. 83, 38 C.H.R.R. D/107 (Fed. T.D.); *Simcoe (County) v. Brewery, General & Professional Workers' Union* (2002), 2002 CarswellOnt 4708, 108 L.A.C. (4th) 254 (Ont. Arb. Bd.)

[4] *Ontario Jockey Club v. S.E.I.U.,* Local 528 (2001), 151 O.A.C. 375, 2001 CarswellOnt 3904, 41 C.H.R.R. D/361 (Ont. Div. Ct.); *Mainland Sawmills v. IWA-Canada,* Local 2171 (2002), 2002 CarswellBC 2465, 104 L.A.C. (4th) 385 (B.C. Arb. Bd.); *Browning v. Saskatchewan* (2002), 2002 CarswellSask 491, 18 C.C.E.L. (3d) 244 (Sask. Human Rights Comm.); *Stevenson v. Canada (Security Intelligence Service)* (2001), 2001 CarswellNat 3503, 2002 C.L.L.C. 230-021, 19 C.C.E.L. (3d) 121, 41 C.H.R.R. D/433 (Can. Human Rights Trib.), reversed on other grounds 2003 CarswellNat 919, 2003 CarswellNat 1616, 2003 FCT 341, 2003 CFPI 431, 229 F.T.R. 297 (Fed. T.D.)

[5] B.C. Human Rights Commission, *The Duty to Accommodate*

[6] *O.N.A. v. Orillia Soldiers Memorial Hospital* (1999), 42 O.R. (3d) 692, 1999 CarswellOnt 28, [1999] O.J. No. 44, 40 C.C.E.L. (2d) 263, 99 C.L.L.C. 230-007, 169 D.L.R. (4th) 489, 117 O.A.C. 146, 20 C.C.P.B. 195, 36 C.H.R.R. D/202 (Ont. C.A.), leave to appeal refused (1999), 252 N.R. 196 (note), [1999] S.C.C.A. No. 118, 133 O.A.C. 199 (note) (S.C.C.); and see, re buyout program, *Starzynski v. Canada Safeway Ltd.* (2000), 2000 CarswellAlta 1473, [2000] A.J. No. 1445, 2000 ABQB 897, [2001] 3 W.W.R. 651, 86 Alta. L.R. (3d) 366, 2001 C.L.L.C. 230-027, 280 A.R. 68, 44 C.H.R.R. D/272 (Alta. Q.B.), affirmed 2003 CarswellAlta 1176, 2003 ABCA 246 (Alta. C.A.) contra: *British Columbia v. B.C.G.E.U.* (2002), 2002 CarswellBC 3316, 109 L.A.C. (4th) 1 (B.C. Arb. Bd.)

[7] B.C. Human Rights Commission, *The Duty to Accommodate*

[8] *Babcock & Wilcox Canada v. U.S.W.A., Local 2859*, 2003 CarswellOnt 1860, [2003] L.V.I. 3359-1 (Ont. Arb. Bd.)

[9] *Pasteur Merieux Connaught Canada v. C.E.P., Local 1701* (1998), 1998 CarswellOnt 5637, 75 L.A.C. (4th) 235 (Ont. Arb. Bd.). In this case, the absences were over a period of 9½ years.

[10] *Babcock & Wilcox Canada v. U.S.W.A., Local 2859*, 2003 CarswellOnt 1860, [2003] L.V.I. 3359-1 (Ont. Arb. Bd.); *Uniroyal Goodrich Canada Inc. v. U.S.W.A., Local 677* (1999), 79 L.A.C. (4th) 129, 1999 CarswellOnt 3451 (Ont. Arb. Bd.). In *Pharma Plus Drugmart Ltd. v. U.F.C.W.* (1993), 33 L.A.C. (4th) 1, 1993 CarswellOnt 1230 (Ont. Arb. Bd.), a duty to accommodate was found after a three-year absence eventhough the employee had neither provided medical information to the employer nor fully communicated the hope of a return to work. In *Thomas Lighting v. U.S.W.A., Local 7607*, 2000 CarswellOnt 4843, [2000] L.V.I. 3158-7 (Ont. Arb. Bd.), the employer was justified in discharging the employee after a five-year period involving the same circumstances. In contrast, in *Abitibi-Price Inc. v. C.P.U.*, Local 90, (1992) 31 L.A.C. (4th) 211 (Ont. Arb. Bd.), where the absence was four years, there was no such duty because the employee was unable to perform any kind of modified work and there was no reasonable prospect of a return to work in the foreseeable future.

[11] *Parisien v. Ottawa-Carlton Transit Comm.*, 2003 CHRT 10 (Can. Human Rights Trib.); B.C. Human Rights Commission, *The Duty to Accommodate*

[12] *Desormeaux v. Ottawa-Carleton Regional Transit Commission*, 2003 CHRT 2, [2003] C.H.R.T. No. 1, 2003 CarswellNat 901 (Can. Human Rights Trib.)

[13] *Ottawa Civic Hospital v. O.N.A.* (1995), 1995 CarswellOnt 1438, 48 L.A.C. (4th) 388 (Ont. Arb. Bd.)

[14] *O.P.S.E.U. v. Ontario (Ministry of Community & Social Services)* (1996), 89 O.A.C. 161, 1996 CarswellOnt 545, [1996] O.J. No. 608, 96 C.L.L.C. 230-016 (Ont. Div. Ct.), leave to appeal refused (1996), 1996 CarswellOnt 4378 (Ont. C.A.); *Maple Leaf Meats Inc. v. U.F.C.W., Locals 175 & 633* (2001), 2001 CarswellOnt 2374, 149 O.A.C. 295 (Ont. Div. Ct.); *Black v. Gaines Pet Foods* (1993), 16 O.R. (3d) 290, 1993 CarswellOnt 967, 50 C.C.E.L. 315, 94 C.L.L.C. 17,004, 28 C.H.R.R. D/256 (Ont. Div. Ct.); *Etobicoke General Hospital v. O.N.A.* (1993), 14 O.R. (3d) 40, 1993 CarswellOnt 1835, 64 O.A.C. 66, 94 C.L.L.C. 17,017, 104 D.L.R. (4th) 379 (Ont. Div. Ct.); *Mainland Sawmills v. IWA-Canada, Local 2171* (2002), 2002 CarswellBC 2465, 104 L.A.C. (4th) 385 (B.C. Arb. Bd.); *Cache Creek (Village) v. I.U.O.E., Local 115C* (2002), 2002 CarswellBC 2482, 105 L.A.C. (4th) 97 (B.C. Arb. Bd.); but see contra: *Brewery, Beverage & Soft Drink Workers, Local 250 v. Labatt's Alberta Brewery* (1996), 1996 CarswellAlta 313, 38 Alta. L.R. (3d) 308, 96 C.L.L.C. 210-035, 184 A.R. 162, 122 W.A.C. 162 (Alta. C.A.)

[15] *C.U.P.W. v. Canada Post Corp.*, 2001 CarswellBC 684, 2001 BCCA 256, 87 B.C.L.R. (3d) 341, 152 B.C.A.C. 24, 250 W.A.C. 24 (B.C. C.A.), leave to appeal refused (2001), 2001 CarswellBC 2058, 2001 CarswellBC 2059, 282 N.R. 199 (note), 165 B.C.A.C. 160 (note), 270 W.A.C. 160 (note) (S.C.C.); *O.P.S.E.U. v. Ontario (Ministry of Community & Social Services)* (1996), 89 O.A.C. 161, 1996 CarswellOnt 545, [1996] O.J. No. 608, 96 C.L.L.C. 230-016 (Ont. Div. Ct.), leave to appeal refused (1996), 1996 CarswellOnt 4378 (Ont. C.A.); *Maple Leaf Meats Inc. v. U.F.C.W., Locals 175 & 633* (2001), 2001 CarswellOnt 2374, 149 O.A.C. 295 (Ont. Div. Ct.); *Black v. Gaines Pet Foods* (1993), 16 O.R. (3d) 290, 1993 CarswellOnt 967, 50 C.C.E.L. 315, 94 C.L.L.C. 17,004, 28 C.H.R.R. D/256 (Ont. Div. Ct.); *Etobicoke General Hospital v. O.N.A.* (1993), 14 O.R. (3d) 40, 1993 CarswellOnt 1835, 64 O.A.C. 66, 94 C.L.L.C. 17,017, 104 D.L.R. (4th) 379 (Ont. Div. Ct.) But see *Canada Post Corp. v. C.U.P.W.*, 2001 CarswellNat 794, [2001] L.V.I. 3193-9 (Can. Arb. Bd.). It was decided that a disabled employee with allergies should have a level of attendance which

is reasonable. This is defined as neither the same as "average" or "excessive" absenteeism.

[16] *C.U.P.E., Local 1582 v. Toronto (Metropolitan) Reference Library Board*, 1995 CarswellOnt 1856, [1995] L.V.I. 2668-6 (Ont. Arb. Bd.)

[17] *Shirley v. Eecol Electric (Sask.) Ltd.* (2001), 2001 CarswellSask 255, 2001 C.L.L.C. 230-021, 39 C.H.R.R. D/168 (Sask. Bd. of Inquiry); *Bielecky v. Young, MacNamara* (1992), 20 C.H.R.R. D/215 (Ont. Bd. of Inquiry); contra: *Marzano v. Nathar Ltd.* (1992), 18 C.H.R.R. D/248 (Ont. Bd. of Inquiry)

◆

CHAPTER 7

REASONABLE ACCOMMODATION AND SUBSTANCE ABUSE

- Pre-Employment
  - Disclosure
  - Testing
- On the Job
  - Disclosure
  - Testing
  - Use or Possession of Drugs or Alcohol
- Accommodating Substance Abuse
  - Last Chance Agreements
  - Duty of the Employer and the Employee
  - Assessing Undue Hardship
- Summary

Increasingly, employers are creating policies regarding alcohol and drugs. However, employers have to keep in mind that drug and alcohol addictions are considered disabilities under human rights law. Casual or recreational use of alcohol or drugs does not constitute a handicap.[1]

As mentioned above, the employer's human rights obligations commence when there is a position to be filled. These duties continue throughout the search for an incumbent; however, they are viewed in a slightly different manner by the human rights commissions. Unions also have responsibilities and they must participate in the development and implementation of a drug and alcohol policy.[2]

Without question, it is a legitimate employer objective to promote workplace safety by minimizing employee substance abuse on the job. It is a *bona fide* occupational requirement that employees are not impaired by alcohol or drugs while working at safety-sensitive jobs.[3] The question is, how can an employer ensure that employees in safety-sensitive jobs are not impaired without breaching human rights laws. Moreover, what is the scope of substance abuse programs for jobs which are not safety-sensitive?[4]

Pre-Employment

Disclosure

There are different views of acceptable questions posed to job applicants regarding substance abuse in the application form and at job interviews.

- According to the Ontario and federal human rights commissions, neither in an application form nor during the job interview can an employer ask about past or present substance abuse or about membership in a medical or patient organization, such as, Alcoholics Anonymous.
- In contrast, with respect to job interviews for safety-sensitive positions, the draft guidelines of the New Brunswick Commission indicate that the employer may require the disclosure of "problems with drugs and alcohol within the past six years".
- The federal, New Brunswick and Ontario Human Rights Commissions indicate that where alcohol or drug testing is a valid requirement of the job due to safety issues, the employer must advise the applicant.[5]

Testing

In 2000, the Ontario Court of Appeal made a decision which changed the law dramatically. In *Entrop*, the court found that pre-employment drug testing is always unacceptable before a job offer has been made and accepted. This is because a positive test does not show future impairment or likely future impairment on the job. With respect to new employees, the rule is different, but only with respect to safety-sensitive positions. In this situation, drug and alcohol testing is acceptable where it is part of a larger assessment to determine whether use is recreational or addictive. No ruling was made regarding pre-employment alcohol testing.[6]

Since the *Entrop* decision, several human rights commissions have developed policies on pre-employment drug and alcohol testing:

- The Canadian and Ontario Human Rights Commissions advise against all pre-employment testing for drugs or alcohol.

- In contrast, the Saskatchewan and New Brunswick Commissions indicate that, after an offer of employment, pre-employment drug and alcohol testing may be permissible with respect to safety-sensitive jobs.
- From the perspective of the New Brunswick Commission, pre-employment testing is appropriate where the job applicant discloses an existing or past abuse problem or a pre-employment medical exam provides reasonable cause to believe the applicant may become impaired on the job.

When a job applicant tests positive, this is not the end of the story. The employer still has a duty to accommodate the applicant and must permit the applicant to reapply or retest the applicant at a later date.[7]

On the Job

Disclosure

Disclosure rules are broader on the job than pre-employment. In Entrop, the Ontario Court of Appeal considered employee disclosure of past drug and alcohol abuse. It found that mandatory reporting is acceptable only with respect to safety-sensitive jobs and must be restricted to incidents which occurred within the previous six years.[8]

As mentioned above, it is important for employers to have in place human resources practices and procedures which alert managers and co-workers to the signs of substance abuse. This is because the employer may be under a duty to accommodate an employee, even where the employee does not disclose a disability which is hidden—that is psychological disabilities, including substance abuse.[9]

Testing

Testing of employees on the job is permissible in several circumstances.

According to the Ontario Court of Appeal decision in Entrop:

- Testing for drugs and/or alcohol is always acceptable after a work accident or because the employee's behaviour suggests substance abuse ("for cause").
- With respect to random testing, however, the rules are different. This is because drug testing technology is not sophisticated enough to measure impairment at the time of testing. Only past drug use can be measured. In contrast, breathalyzer tests measure impairment

from alcohol at the time of the test. Thus, employers can require employees in safety-sensitive positions to undergo random testing for alcohol, but only where supervision is limited.

- Random testing for drugs is never acceptable, according to the *Entrop* decision. However, recent decisions of the B.C. and Ontario Arbitration Boards have permitted random drug testing.[10]

The human rights commissions have approached this issue in various ways:

- The federal and New Brunswick Human Rights Commissions permit periodic or random testing following disclosure of a current drug or alcohol abuse problem.
- Least restrictive of the Human Rights Commission policies is that of Saskatchewan. It permits drug and alcohol testing where an employer, acting honestly and in good faith, uses it for a purpose which is rationally connected to the performance of the job and where testing is reasonably necessary for the fulfillment of a work-related purpose.
- Alternatives to drug and alcohol testing are emphasized in the policies of the federal, New Brunswick and Ontario Human Rights Commissions. This would include functional performance testing to determine impairment of an employee's ability to perform the essential duties of the job. From the point of view of the Ontario Commission, testing for the presence of drugs and alcohol in the body is not reasonable.[11]

Use or Possession of Drugs or Alcohol

Recently, a British Columbia Human Rights Tribunal found that a policy which imposes sanctions on employees who possess or consume drugs or alcohol on the job is not discriminatory; it is not directed at identifying all employees who use drugs or alcohol, but at prohibiting specific behaviour on the job.[12] The Saskatchewan Human Rights Commissions permits an employer to prohibit possession or use of illegal drugs and alcohol in the workplace.[13]

Accommodating Substance Abuse

Last Chance Agreements

Ontario courts have refused to enforce last chance agreements signed by employees with disabilities because the employer failed to show it was unable to accommodate the employee short of undue hardship.[14] They have indicated that neither employees nor employers can contract out of human rights legislation and last chance agreements are subject to the duty to accommodate.

However, in reviewing last chance agreements signed by employees with substance abuse problems, Ontario labour arbitrators have sometimes interpreted last chance agreements, themselves, as a form of accommodation by the employer, rather than a contracting out of human rights obligations. Moreover, Ontario arbitrators have considered the actions of the employer before the last chance agreement was signed.[15] Also relevant is whether the employee recognized at the time of signing the agreement that substance abuse was the root of the problem.[16] The question is, whether there is anything else the employer could do without undue hardship.

Duty of the Employer and Employee

If an employee's alcohol or drug test result is positive, the employer is normally required to provide reasonable accommodation, particularly where this is the employee's first such incident. The employee is also under a duty to undergo random testing for a reasonable period of time, or dismissal is justified.[17]

Moreover, sanctions must not be more severe than is necessary for a safe workplace and must be individually tailored to the employee's circumstances. The strict application of sanctions or standards, such as termination, reassignment or two years of rehabilitation, is not acceptable. Where appropriate, the employer must permit an employee to undergo a rehabilitation program and retain employee status.[18]

An employee disabled by alcoholism and/or drug addiction must take reasonable steps to obtain treatment.[19] But employers have no obligation to diagnose and force treatment upon employees who fail to reveal that alcoholism is the reason for their extensive absenteeism when they consent to a last chance agreement.[20]

47

People addicted to drugs and/or alcohol frequently deny their addiction and have difficulty coming to terms with it. Relapse is the norm. Moreover, these addictions can often lead to compulsive behaviour or workplace misconduct. In assessing what is reasonable accommodation, employers must include these features of the illness.[21] The employer must allow reasonable time for the employee to confront the alcoholism and assist in that endeavour.[22]

The least the employer should do is allow the employee a leave of absence to address the addiction and pay disability benefits which would be the same as those paid for other types of disability. During the time off, the employee should maintain regular contact with the employer.[23]

Assessing Undue Hardship

The extent of the employer's obligation to accommodate an alcoholic employee depends on:

- The efforts of the employer in the past.
- The length of time the employee has spent with the company.
- The effect of the employee's absence on the workplace.
- The employee's prospects for success at abstaining.
- Employer cost factors.
- Short term sick leave benefits already paid for substance abuse.
- Monitoring compliance with conditions of reinstatement.
- Substance abuse treatment.
- Burden to the employer due to a relapse after reinstatement.
- History of discipline and absenteeism for substance abuse.
- Past leaves of absence for substance abuse rehabilitation programs.
- Whether the employer accommodated return to work hours to meet the rehabilitation program requirements.[24]

An employer does not have the duty to indefinitely accommodate an alcoholic employee in terms of leaves of absence and access to weekly indemnity benefits. If the employee does not accept or access available treatment over an extended period, discharge is acceptable. Moreover, the employer is entitled to objective evidence of fitness before readmitting the employee to the workplace.[25]

Summary

How employers deal with substance abuse has been extremely contentious, producing many tribunal and court decisions in the last few years. Without question, it is a legitimate employer objective to promote workplace safety by minimizing employee substance abuse on the job. However, the focus is safety, and with respect to positions which are not safety-sensitive, the employer has much less scope.

At the pre-employment stage, disclosure of substance abuse is rarely acceptable—the same is true of testing. On the job, employers have more scope to require disclosure and testing, particularly in safety-sensitive jobs. Where safety is not an issue, testing is acceptable after a work accident or where the employee's behaviour suggests substance abuse. However, there is some variation across Canada, according to human rights commission policies.

As is true of all other disabilities, the employer must accommodate substance abuse. People addicted to drugs or alcohol frequently deny their addiction and have difficulty coming to terms with it. Relapse is the norm. This is taken into account in considering the duty to accommodate. Moreover, sanctions must be individually tailored to the employee's circumstances. Nonetheless, the employee has to take reasonable steps to obtain treatment.

ENDNOTES

[1] *Entrop v. Imperial Oil Ltd.* (2000), 2 C.C.E.L. (3d) 19, 2000 Carswel-lOnt 2525, [2000] O.J. No. 2689, 189 D.L.R. (4th) 14, 50 O.R. (3d) 18, 2000 C.L.L.C. 230-037, 137 O.A.C. 15, 37 C.H.R.R. D/481 (Ont. C.A.). For information on developing drug and alcohol policies, see Butler, B., "Issues Consideration when Introducing Alcohol and Drug Testing" in Butler et al. *The Drug Testing Controversy.* Toronto: Carswell, 1997.

[2] *DuPont Canada Inc. v. C.E.P., Local 28-O*, 2002 CarswellOnt 1739, [2002] L.V.I. 3282-1, 105 L.A.C. (4th) 399 (Ont. Arb. Bd.)

[3] *Entrop v. Imperial Oil Ltd.* (2000), 2 C.C.E.L. (3d) 19, 2000 Carswell-Ont 2525, [2000] O.J. No. 2689, 189 D.L.R. (4th) 14, 50 O.R. (3d) 18, 2000 C.L.L.C. 230-037, 137 O.A.C. 15, 37 C.H.R.R. D/481 (Ont. C.A.).

[4] See Fishbein & Williamson, "Random Alcohol and Drug Testing" and Lynck, "Accommodation, Disability and the Unionized Canadian Workplace" in *Human Rights in the Unionized Workplace*, CBAO Continuing Legal Education, 2001

[5] See Appendix B: Ontario Human Rights Commission, *Drug and Alcohol Testing*; New Brunswick Human Rights Commission, *Draft Guideline on Drug and Alcohol Testing in the Workplace*

[6] *Entrop v. Imperial Oil Ltd.* (2000), 2 C.C.E.L. (3d) 19, 2000 CarswellOnt 2525, [2000] O.J. No. 2689, 189 D.L.R. (4th) 14, 50 O.R. (3d) 18, 2000 C.L.L.C. 230-037, 137 O.A.C. 15, 37 C.H.R.R. D/481 (Ont. C.A.); see also *Canadian Civil Liberties Assn. v. Toronto Dominion Bank*, [1998] F.C.J. No. 1036, 1998 CarswellNat 1352, 1998 CarswellNat 2708, 98 C.L.L.C. 230-030, 229 N.R. 135, 163 D.L.R. (4th) 193, 38 C.C.E.L. (2d) 8, 32 C.H.R.R. D/261, [1998] 4 F.C. 205, 154 F.T.R. 101 (note) (Fed. C.A.)

[7] See Appendix B: Canadian Human Rights Commission, *Policy on Alcohol and Drug Testing*; New Brunswick Human Rights Commission, *Drug and Alcohol Testing (Draft)*; Ontario Human Rights Commission, *Drug and Alcohol Testing*; Saskatchewan Human Rights Commission, *Policy Statement on Drug and Alcohol Testing* and see British Columbia Human Rights Commission, *Disability — Dependence on Alcohol, Disability — Dependence on Drugs*

[8] *Entrop v. Imperial Oil Ltd.* (2000), 2 C.C.E.L. (3d) 19, 2000 CarswellOnt 2525, [2000] O.J. No. 2689, 189 D.L.R. (4th) 14, 50 O.R. (3d) 18, 2000 C.L.L.C. 230-037, 137 O.A.C. 15, 37 C.H.R.R. D/481 (Ont. C.A.)

[9] *Cache Creek (Village) v. I.U.O.E., Local 115C* (2002), 2002 CarswellBC 2482, 105 L.A.C. (4th) 97 (B.C. Arb. Bd.); *Mainland Sawmills v. IWA-Canada, Local 2171* (2002), 2002 CarswellBC 2465, 104 L.A.C. (4th) 385 (B.C. Arb. Bd.); *Ottawa Civic Hospital v. O.N.A.* (1995), 1995 CarswellOnt 1438, 48 L.A.C. (4th) 388 (Ont. Arb. Bd.); and see above, Chapter 3 The Duty of the Employee, Employer and Union

[10] *Cache Creek (Village) v. I.U.O.E., Local 115C* (2002), 2002 CarswellBC 2482, 105 L.A.C. (4th) 97 (B.C. Arb. Bd.); *DuPont Canada Inc. v. C.E.P., Local 28-O*, 2002 CarswellOnt 1739, [2002] L.V.I. 3282-1, 105 L.A.C. (4th) 399 (Ont. Arb. Bd.)

[11] Appendix B: Canadian Human Rights Commission, *Drug and Alcohol Testing*; New Brunswick Human Rights Commission, *Drug and Alco-*

hol Testing (Draft); Ontario Human Rights Commission, *Drug and Alcohol Testing*; Saskatchewan Human Rights Commission, *Drug and Alcohol Testing*

[12] *Middlemiss v. Norske Canada Ltd.*, 2002 CarswellBC 2014, 2002 C.L.L.C. 230-024, 2002 BCHRT 5 (B.C. Human Rights Trib.)

[13] Appendix B: Saskatchewan Human Rights Commission, *Drug and Alcohol Testing*. So did the British Columbia Human Rights Commission, which has since been abolished; see *Disability — Dependence on Drugs*; *Disability — Dependence on Alcohol*.

[14] *O.P.S.E.U. v. Ontario (Ministry of Community & Social Services)* (1996), 89 O.A.C. 161, 1996 CarswellOnt 545, [1996] O.J. No. 608, 96 C.L.L.C. 230-016 (Ont. Div. Ct.), leave to appeal refused (1996), 1996 CarswellOnt 4378 (Ont. C.A.)

[15] *Frost Wire Products Ltd. v. U.S.W.A., Local 3561*, 1998 CarswellOnt 4598, [1998] L.V.I. 2951-1 (Ont. Arb. Bd.); *Toronto District School Board v. C.U.P.E.* (1999), 79 L.A.C. (4th) 365, 1999 CarswellOnt 3230 (Ont. Arb. Bd.); *Norbord Industries Inc. v. IWA-Canada, Local 1-2995* (1997), 1997 CarswellOnt 5652, 67 L.A.C. (4th) 205 (Ont. Arb. Bd.)

[16] *Ottawa Civic Hospital v. O.N.A.* (1995), 1995 CarswellOnt 1438, 48 L.A.C. (4th) 388 (Ont. Arb. Bd.); *Labatt Breweries Ontario v. Brewery, General & Professional Workers' Union, Local 304* (2002), 2002 CarswellOnt 4688, 107 L.A.C. (4th) 126 (Ont. Arb. Bd.)*; Cache Creek (Village) v. I.U.O.E., Local 115C* (2002), 2002 CarswellBC 2482, 105 L.A.C. (4th) 97 (B.C. Arb. Bd.); *Norbord Industries Inc. v. IWA-Canada, Local 1-2995* (1997), 1997 CarswellOnt 5652, 67 L.A.C. (4th) 205 (Ont. Arb. Bd.), Jarvis & Meier, "Last Chance Agreements: Still Alive and Well?" in *Human Rights in the Unionized Workplace*, C.B.A.O. Continuing Legal Education: 2001

[17] *DuPont Canada Inc. v. C.E.P., Local 28-O*, 2002 CarswellOnt 1739, [2002] L.V.I. 3282-1, 105 L.A.C. (4th) 399 (Ont. Arb. Bd.)

[18] *Entrop v. Imperial Oil Ltd.* (2000), 2 C.C.E.L. (3d) 19, 2000 CarswellOnt 2525, [2000] O.J. No. 2689, 189 D.L.R. (4th) 14, 50 O.R. (3d) 18, 2000 C.L.L.C. 230-037, 137 O.A.C. 15, 37 C.H.R.R. D/481 (Ont. C.A.)

[19] *Uniroyal Goodrich Canada Inc. v. U.S.W.A., Local 677* (1999), 79 L.A.C. (4th) 129, 1999 CarswellOnt 3451 (Ont. Arb. Bd.); *Toronto District School Board v. C.U.P.E.* (1999), 1999 CarswellOnt 3230, 79 L.A.C. (4th) 365 (Ont. Arb. Bd.)

[20] *Frost Wire Products Ltd. v. U.S.W.A., Local 3561*, 1998 CarswellOnt 4598, [1998] L.V.I. 2951-1 (Ont. Arb. Bd.); *Toronto District School Board v. C.U.P.E.* (1999), 79 L.A.C. (4th) 365, 1999 CarswellOnt 3230 (Ont. Arb. Bd.)

[21] *Labatt Breweries Ontario v. Brewery, General & Professional Workers' Union, Local 304* (2002), 2002 CarswellOnt 4688, 107 L.A.C. (4th) 126 (Ont. Arb. Bd.); *British Columbia v. B.C.G.S.E.U.* (2002), 2002 CarswellBC 3338 (B.C. L.R.B.); Lynk, S., "Accommodation, Disability and the Unionized Canadian Workplace" in *Human Rights in the Unionized Workplace*, C.B.A.O., Continuing Legal Education: 2001

[22] *British Columbia v. B.C.G.S.E.U.* (2002), 2002 CarswellBC 3338 (B.C. L.R.B.)

[23] *Mainland Sawmills v. IWA-Canada, Local 2171* (2002), 2002 CarswellBC 2465, 104 L.A.C. (4th) 385 (B.C. Arb. Bd.); *Browning v. Saskatchewan* (2002), 2002 CarswellSask 491, 18 C.C.E.L. (3d) 244 (Sask. Human Rights Comm.)

[24] *Cache Creek (Village) v. I.U.O.E., Local 115C* (2002), 2002 CarswellBC 2482, 105 L.A.C. (4th) 97 (B.C. Arb. Bd.); *Labatt Breweries Ontario v. Brewery, General & Professional Workers' Union, Local 304* (2002), 2002 CarswellOnt 4688, 107 L.A.C. (4th) 126 (Ont. Arb. Bd.); *Norbord Industries Inc. v. IWA-Canada, Local 1-2995* (1997), 1997 CarswellOnt 5652, 67 L.A.C. (4th) 205 (Ont. Arb. Bd.); *Toronto District School Board v. C.U.P.E.* (1999), 1999 CarswellOnt 3230, 79 L.A.C. (4th) 365 (Ont. Arb. Bd.); *Ottawa Civic Hospital v. O.N.A.* (1995), 1995 CarswellOnt 1438, 48 L.A.C. (4th) 388 (Ont. Arb. Bd.); Jarvis & Meier, "Last Chance Agreements: Still Alive and Well?" in *Human Rights in the Unionized Workplace*, C.B.A.O. Continuing Legal Education: 2001. A one-time relapse by an employee who previously had his alcoholism under control for 17 years does not justify dismissal after the employer has made one effort to accommodate the employee and the employee has failed to respond successfully. See *C.E.P., Local 305 v. International Wallcoverings Ltd.*, 1998 CarswellOnt 2074, [1998] L.V.I. 2927-2 (Ont. Arb. Bd.)

[25] *Uniroyal Goodrich Canada Inc. v. U.S.W.A., Local 677* (1999), 1999 CarswellOnt 3451, 79 L.A.C. (4th) 129 (Ont. Arb. Bd.); *C.E.P., Local 305 v. International Wallcoverings Ltd.*, 1998 CarswellOnt 2074, [1998] L.V.I. 2927-2 (Ont. Arb. Bd.)

◆

CHAPTER 8

DISCHARGE

- Last Chance Agreement
- Absence from Work
- Collective Agreement
- Summary

If a disabled employee is unable to perform the essential duties of their pre-disability job, discharge may be justified, subject to the employer's duty to accommodate. Therefore, employers must document any difficulties a disabled employee has in performing essential job tasks. Proper employment practices are essential for both fair treatment of employees and for documentation of job performance difficulties. Employers also need to record all efforts made to accommodate a disabled employee and provide this information to the employee.[1]

As a general rule, if discrimination is one reason for dismissal, there is a breach of human rights law. Thus, if an employee's absences are caused partly by a disability, the employer has a duty to accommodate the disability; otherwise, discharge may result in a finding of discrimination.[2] At the same time, an employee's disability does not protect him or her from discharge due to improper conduct, poor job performance or innocent absenteeism.[3] However, the discharge of a disabled employee, for whatever reason, must be implemented in accordance with the employer's duty to accommodate the employee. Moreover, when an employee returns from an absence due to a disability, the employer cannot dismiss the employee without a proper assessment.[4]

The following will assist employers in human rights compliance in relation to discharge:
- Provide a range of opportunities to address performance issues on an individualized basis.

- Practice progressive performance management and discipline.
- Develop employee assistance programs.
- Develop disability management programs to track the reasons employees take sick leaves, personal days off and casual absence.
- Inform all employees that a disability-related assessment or accommodation can be provided as an option to address performance issues.
- Train managers to take note when an employee is showing signs of distress and consider whether the problem is a psychological disability or substance abuse.[5]

Last Chance Agreements

Last chance agreements are frequently used to address job performance and absences related to a disability. As mentioned above, employers cannot require employees to forego their rights under human rights legislation.[6] Nor can employees voluntarily contract out of these rights. Thus, restrictive conditions or last chance agreements relating to disability are subject to the duty to accommodate. The duty to accommodate requires the employer to recognize the nature of the employee's problem, allow sufficient time for the problem to be corrected and take all reasonable steps to assist the employee to correct the problem. This means that, in a human rights grievance or complaint, the main issues are the extent to which the employer has accommodated the employee in the past, the role the last chance agreement plays in that accommodation and whether post-breach accommodation is reasonable without undue hardship to the employer. Relevant to this is whether employee absences have caused undue hardship to the employer. In addition, the capacity of the employee to meet reasonable conditions of work performance is important.[7]

Last chance agreements permit the parties to set out the expectations of both the employer and the employee and define just cause for dismissal. They give an employee the opportunity to correct an underlying problem while maintaining employment status; the employer has a measure of certainty with respect to the employee's capacity to work. These agreements should be signed by the employee, the employer and, in a unionized workplace, the union. The parties should address the following issues:

- The nature of the employee's disability and the problems related to work performance,
- The steps the employer has taken to assist the employee with the problem,

- Undertakings of the employee to take particular steps regarding medical treatment of the problem,
- Undertakings of the employer regarding steps it will take to assist the employee,
- Conditions of continued employment,
- The consequences of breach by the employee and
- The expiry date.[8]

It should be noted that last chance agreements which restrict the jurisdiction of an arbitrator will not necessarily be enforced, if the agreement is discriminatory.[9]

Absence from Work

Where there is no medical evidence that an employee will be able to return to regular attendance in the foreseeable future, employers have the right to terminate employees for excessive absenteeism related to disability.[10] An employer who deals with the absenteeism of a disabled employee by requiring a certain level of attendance can expect this standard to be subject to the duty to accommodate, whether the requirement is contained in a collective agreement, last chance agreement or otherwise.[11]

In addition, where accommodation of work absences is not possible without undue hardship to the employer, the employer must be careful to provide to the disabled employee the same procedural rights to which other employees are entitled. In a unionized environment, this means that the employee must have access to the just cause provision of the collective agreement.[12]

Collective Agreement

A clause in a collective agreement which terminates employment due to absence from work for more than 24 months, because of illness or disability, is subject to the employer's duty to accommodate.[13] The same is true of a clause which permits termination of an employee who has exhausted long-term disability benefits.[14] Moreover, human rights law applies to probationary employees. Thus, an article of a collective agreement which prohibits discrimination in the discharge of employees because of handicap applies to disabled probationary employees.[15]

Summary

Discharge is sometimes the only viable option. It is particularly appropriate where the employee has experienced long-term or frequent intermittent absences, if the prognosis for recovery is poor and/or where the employer has experienced significant financial outlays for disability benefits.

Like the rest of employer-employee relations, the discharge stage is subject to the duty to accommodate. Accordingly, last chance agreements will be assessed according to this standard. If discharge is necessary, the employer must provide the disabled employee the same procedural rights to which other employees are entitled.

ENDNOTES

[1] See Carswell *Best Practices* publications: *Performance Management, HR Forms Toolkit,* and *Termination.*

[2] *Velenosi v. Dominion Management* (1997), 148 D.L.R. (4th) 575, 1997 CarswellOnt 1281 (Ont. C.A.); *Desormeaux v. Ottawa-Carleton Regional Transit Commission,* 2003 CHRT 2, [2003] C.H.R.T. No. 1, 2003 CarswellNat 901 (Can. Human Rights Trib.)

[3] *Chinook Health Region v. U.N.A., Local 89* (2002), 2002 CarswellAlta 1762, 110 L.A.C. (4th) 27 (Alta. Arb. Bd.); *CAW-Canada, Local 4501 v. Taylor Ford Sales Ltd.* (2000), 2000 CarswellNB 185, 2000 C.L.L.C. 220-057, 227 N.B.R. (2d) 54, 583 A.P.R. 54 (N.B. Q.B.); *British Columbia v. B.C.G.S.E.U.* (2002), 2002 CarswellBC 3338 (B.C. L.R.B.)

[4] *Chamberlin v. 599273 Ontario Ltd.* (1989), 11 C.H.R.R. D/110 (Ont. Bd. of Inquiry)

[5] *Cache Creek (Village) v. I.U.O.E., Local 115C* (2002), 2002 CarswellBC 2482, 105 L.A.C. (4th) 97 (B.C. Arb. Bd.); *Sylvester v. British Columbia Society of Male Survivors of Sexual Abuse,* 2002 CarswellBC 3216 2003 C.L.L.C. 230-004, 2002 BCHRT 14, 43 C.H.R.R. D/55 (B.C. Human Rights Trib.); *Mainland Sawmills v. IWA-Canada, Local 2171* (2002), 2002 CarswellBC 2465, 104 L.A.C. (4th) 385 (B.C. Arb. Bd.); *Grober Inc. v. U.F.C.W., Local 175* (2002), 2002 CarswellOnt 4763, 109 L.A.C. (4th) 53 (Ont. Arb. Bd.); *Ottawa Civic Hospital v. O.N.A.* (1995), 1995 CarswellOnt 1438, 48 L.A.C. (4th) 388 (Ont. Arb. Bd.); Ontario Human Rights Commission, *Dis-*

ability and the Duty to Accommodate; Galt & Harding. "No safety in the numbers." *Globe and Mail* June 18, 2003

6   See above, Chapter 6 Absence From Work.

7   *Slater Steels v. U.S.W.A., Local 4752* (1998), 76 L.A.C. (4th) 241, 1998 CarswellOnt 5640 (Ont. Arb. Bd.); Jarvis & Meier in "Last Chance Agreements: Still Alive and Well?" in *Human Rights in the Unionized Workplace,* C.B.A.O. Continuing Legal Education: 2001.

8   See Jarvis & Meier in "Last Chance Agreements: Still Alive and Well?" in *Human Rights in the Unionized Workplace*, C.B.A.O. Continuing Legal Education: 2001.

9   *Slater Steels v. U.S.W.A., Local 4752* (1998), 76 L.A.C. (4th) 241, 1998 CarswellOnt 5640 (Ont. Arb. Bd.)

10 *Babcock & Wilcox Canada v. U.S.W.A., Local 2859,* 2002 CarswellOnt 1740, [2002] L.V.I. 3282-3 (Ont. Arb. Bd.); see also *AFG Industries Ltd. v. A.B.G.W.I.U., Local 295G* (1997), 1997 CarswellOnt 5642, 68 L.A.C. (4th) 129 (Ont. Arb. Bd.)

11 *O.P.S.E.U. v. Ontario (Ministry of Community & Social Services)* (1996), 89 O.A.C. 161, 1996 CarswellOnt 545, [1996] O.J. No. 608, 96 C.L.L.C. 230-016 (Ont. Div. Ct.); leave to appeal refused (1966), 1996 CarswellOnt 4378 (Ont. C.A.); *Chinook Health Region v. U.N.A., Local 89* (2002), 2002 CarswellAlta 1762, 110 L.A.C. (4th) 27 (Alta. Arb. Bd.) But see contra: *Brewery, Beverage & Soft Drink Workers, Local 250 v. Labatt's Alberta Brewery* (1996), 1996 CarswellAlta 313, 38 Alta. L.R. (3d) 308, 96 C.L.L.C. 210-035, 184 A.R. 162, 122 W.A.C. 162 (Alta. C.A.); *Canada Post Corp. v. C.U.P.W.,* 2001 CarswellNat 794, [2001] L.V.I. 3193-9 (Can. Arb. Bd.)

12 *Maple Leaf Meats Inc. v. U.F.C.W., Locals 175 & 633* (2001), 2001 CarswellOnt 2374, 149 O.A.C. 295 (Ont. Div. Ct.); *O.P.S.E.U. v. Ontario (Ministry of Community & Social Services)* (1996), 1996 CarswellOnt 545, [1996] O.J. No. 608, 96 C.L.L.C. 230-016, 89 O.A.C. 161 (Ont. Div. Ct.), leave to appeal refused (1996), 1996 CarswellOnt 4378 (Ont. C.A.); *Black v. Gaines Pet Foods* (1993), 1993 CarswellOnt 967, 50 C.C.E.L. 315, 94 C.L.L.C. 17,004, 16 O.R. (3d) 290, 28 C.H.R.R. D/256 (Ont. Div. Ct.); *Etobicoke General Hospital v. O.N.A.* (1993), 94 C.L.L.C. 17,017, 1993 CarswellOnt 1835, 14 O.R. (3d) 40, 64 O.A.C. 66, 104 D.L.R. (4th) 379 (Ont. Div. Ct.)

[13] *Etobicoke General Hospital v. O.N.A.* (1993), 14 O.R. (3d) 40, 94 C.L.L.C. 17,017, 1993 CarswellOnt 1835, 64 O.A.C. 66, 104 D.L.R. (4th) 379 (Ont. Div. Ct.)

[14] *Chinook Health Region v. U.N.A., Local 89* (2002), 2002 CarswellAlta 1762, 110 L.A.C. (4th) 27 (Alta. Arb. Bd.)

[15] *Dominion Castings Ltd. v. U.S.W.A., Local 9392* (1998), 1998 CarswellOnt 5515, 73 L.A.C. (4th) 347 (Ont. Arb. Bd.)

◆
CHAPTER 9

CONCLUSION

The basis of effective accommodation of a disability is a broad spectrum of human resources policies and practices which clarify job duties, provide progressive performance management, train managers in human rights and provide employee support.

This is because the employer's duty to accommodate applies to the entire employment process, starting with the job description. The crux of human rights law as it relates to disability is whether the disabled employee can, within a reasonable period of time, perform the essential duties of the pre-disability job or an available job. To address this, employers must have in place a complete set of job descriptions defined to comply with human rights law—that is, organized into essential and non-essential duties.

The most effective approach to accommodating disability in the workplace is proactive, based on human resource programs which anticipate possible human rights problems. The employer who provides a range of opportunities to address performance issues on an individualized basis will be on firm ground in addressing disability issues. Most employers have progressive performance assessment and discipline. A disability-related assessment or accommodation can be provided as an option to address performance issues. Apart from providing employee assistance supports, employers need disability management programs to track the reasons employees take sick leaves, personal days off and casual absences. Moreover, as part of their human rights training, managers can learn to recognize when an employee is showing signs of distress and consider whether the problem is a psychological disability or substance abuse.

When a request for accommodation is made, the employee should identify their needs and limitations related to the disability. The employee must co-operate with the employer in reviewing options to accommodate and, in a unionized environment, discussions must include the union. Nonetheless, the onus is on the employer because it has the best information about the workplace and the job options available.

In accommodating a disabled employee, it is clear that the employer is expected to accept hardship. But the hardship should not be "undue". Gauging how much hardship is "undue" is difficult. It would appear that the standard is very high, that the employer is expected to investigate all possible options to accommodate a disabled employee. This far surpasses minor inconvenience.

Several factors are relevant in determining undue hardship. The most important of these, for most employers, is the cost of the available options. This is linked to other factors, such as the size of the operation, disruption of operations, and interchangeability of the workforce and facilities. The interests of co-workers are also relevant. These interests include employee morale and rights under employment legislation, and particularly in a unionized environment, the collective agreement. In some cases, the most important factor is safety; not merely of the disabled employee, but also co-workers, patients, customers and the general public.

Most accommodation falls within either changes to the work environment or job duties. Sometimes, what is necessary is a flexible work schedule or part-time hours. But if that is not enough, a complete work absence for recuperation may be necessary.

The key is balance. In each case, the relevant factors will vary, as will their importance. It is not possible to formulate a rule because each assessment must be individual. What is possible for a government employer may not be possible for a small private company. It is a matter of considering the harm to the disabled employee caused by not implementing the accommodation in terms of the hardship caused by its implementation.

◆

APPENDIX A

COMMON LAW HUMAN RIGHTS STATUTES

Alberta — *Human Rights, Citizenship and Multiculturalism Act*
British Columbia — *Human Rights Code*
Canada — *Canadian Human Rights Act*
Manitoba — *Human Rights Code*
New Brunswick — *Human Rights Act*
Newfoundland — *Newfoundland Human Rights Code*
Nova Scotia — *Human Rights Act*
Ontario — *Human Rights Code*
Prince Edward Island — *Human Rights Act*
Saskatchewan — *Saskatchewan Human Rights Code*
Yukon — *Human Rights Act*

◆
APPENDIX B

ABRIDGED
HUMAN RIGHTS COMMISSION POLICIES
ON DISABILITY

Alberta
Duty to Accommodate (2002)

Federal
Alcohol and Drug Testing (2002)

New Brunswick
Drug and Alcohol Testing (Draft)

Ontario
Disability and the Duty to Accommodate (2002)
Drug and Alcohol Testing (2002)

Saskatchewan
Drug and Alcohol Testing (2002)

♦

ALBERTA HUMAN RIGHTS COMMISSION

DUTY TO ACCOMMODATE (2002)

Accommodation means making changes to certain rules, standards, policies, workplace cultures and physical environments to ensure that they don't have a negative effect on a person because of the person's mental or physical disability, religion, gender or any other protected ground.

Accommodation is a way to balance the diverse needs of individuals, groups, organizations and businesses in our society. It may cause a degree of inconvenience, disruption and expense. Accommodation is not a nicety or a courtesy—it is required by law.

To What Extent is Accommodation Required?

The Supreme Court of Canada has ruled that employers and unions have a legal duty to take reasonable steps to accommodate individual needs to the point of undue hardship. To substantiate a claim of undue hardship, an employer must show that they would experience more than a minor inconvenience. In many cases, accommodation measures are simple and affordable and do not create undue hardship.

What is Undue Hardship?

Undue hardship occurs if accommodation would create onerous conditions for an employer, for example, intolerable financial costs or serious disruption to business. To determine if undue hardship would occur, the employer or service provider should review factors such as:

Financial costs: Financial costs must be substantial in order to be found to cause undue hardship. They must be so significant that they would substantially affect productivity or efficiency of the employer responsible for the accommodation. Accommodation measures could result in lost revenue, which should be taken into account when assessing undue hardship. However, if lost revenue due to accommodation would be offset by increased productivity, tax exemptions, grants, subsidies or other gains, then undue hardship may not be a factor. Financial costs do not include the expense of complying with other legislation or regulations, such as building codes (for example, providing wheelchair accessible washrooms).

Size and resources of the employer: The ability of the employer to absorb the cost of modifying premises or equipment (particularly if firm plans exist to move to more accessible premises) and the ability to amortize such costs. The larger the operation, the more likely it is that it can afford to support a wider range of accommodation for a person seeking accommodation.

Disruption of operations: The extent to which the inconvenience would prevent the employer from carrying out essential business. For example, modifying a workspace in a way that substantially interferes with workflow may be considered too disruptive.

Morale problems of other employees brought about by the accommodation: These could be due to reasons such as the negative impact of increased workload and working too much overtime, including sleep difficulties or other health issues.

Substantial interference with the rights of other individuals or groups: A proposed accommodation should not interfere significantly with the rights of others or discriminate against them. The objections of others must be based on well-grounded concerns that their rights will be affected. For example, a substantial departure from the terms of a collective agreement could be a serious concern.

Interchangeability of work force and facilities: Whether an employer to service provider could relocate employees to other positions on a temporary or permanent basis. This may be easier for a larger company.

Health and safety concerns: Where safety is a concern, consider the level of risk and who bears that risk. For example, consider if the accommodation would violate health and safety regulations.

In employment situations, the following expenses are not normally considered to constitute undue hardship:

• overtime or leave costs that the employer can tolerably bear

- expenses incurred to respond to a grievance or minor disruption to a collective agreement.

While certain accommodation measures may create an undue hardship for one employer, the same measures may not pose an undue hardship for a different employer. For example, the manager of a business with 3 employees may not be able to accommodate a request for revised work hours as easily as a manager who has 25 employees.

Keep in mind that measures that do not cause an employer undue hardship now, may do so in the future if its circumstances change. For example, a company that has recently laid off 50% of their staff due to an economic downturn may no longer be able to accommodate a new request for a change in job duties from an employee with a disability, although the company may have accommodated such requests in the past.

Accommodating Persons with Disabilities

Many complaints about accommodation relate to the grounds of physical and mental disability.

The *Act* says that **physical disability** means "any degree of physical disability, infirmity, malformation or disfigurement that is caused by bodily injury, birth defect or illness." Some disabilities that have been established as protected under human rights law are: epilepsy/seizures, heart attack/heart condition, cancer, severe seasonal allergies, shoulder or back injury, asthma, Crohn's disease, hypertension, hysterectomy, spinal malformation, visual acuity, colour blindness, loss of body parts such as fingers, speech impediments, arthritis, muscular atrophy, cerebral palsy, alcoholism, and drug dependence. Common conditions such as colds and flu that don't last long and have no long-term effects are not normally considered to be physical disabilities.

Mental disabilities are defined by the *Act* as "any mental disorder, developmental disorder or learning disorder, regardless of the cause or duration of the disorder." Some examples of mental disabilities include: dyslexia, depression, schizophrenia, obsessive compulsive disorder and panic attacks.

It is not possible to provide a complete list of conditions normally considered to be disabling under human rights law. The disabilities listed above are examples only.

Rights and Responsibilities in the Accommodation Process

Both the person seeking accommodation and the employer have rights and responsibilities in the accommodation process. The most effective accommodation measures are a result of cooperation and clear communication between both parties.

Rights and Responsibilities of the Person Seeking Accommodation

- Bring the situation to the attention of the employer, preferably in writing. Include the following information:
  - Explain why accommodation is required (for example, because of disability, religious belief, pregnancy, family status, etc.).
  - Support the request for accommodation with evidence or documents (for example, a written statement from a health care provider).
  - Be specific about the need for accommodation and identify personal limitations. Individuals who share a characteristic such as impaired vision often have different needs. Therefore, it is important to indicate exactly what your individual needs are.
  - Suggest appropriate accommodation measures.
  - Indicate how long accommodation will be required, if known.
- Allow a reasonable amount of time for the employer to reply to the request for accommodation.
- Listen to and consider any reasonable accommodation options that the employer proposes.
- Consult an expert such as a human rights officer, human resources officer, union representative or lawyer if it is difficult to determine if the proposed options are reasonable.
- Request details of the cost or other factors creating undue hardship, if the employer indicates that accommodation would pose an undue hardship. Provide more details about your needs if such information is helpful.
- Make a formal agreement with the employer, preferably in writing.
- Cooperate to make the agreement work. Advise the employer of changes in accommodation needs and attempt to agree on a modified accommodation arrangement.
- Be willing to review and modify the accommodation agreement if circumstances or needs change and the agreement is no longer working.
- Tell the employer if the need to accommodate ends.

Rights and Responsibilities of the Employer

- Determine if the request falls under any of the areas and grounds protected under the *Act*. Be aware that the onus to accommodate is on the employer, once a request is received.
- Respect the dignity and privacy of the person or group requesting accommodation. Listen to and consider the needs of the person seeking accommodation and their suggestions for accommodation.
- Review any evidence that the person seeking accommodation provides to support the request for accommodation, for example, medical documents.
- Be willing to take substantial and meaningful measures to accommodate the needs of the person seeking accommodation.
- Consult an expert such as a human rights officer, human resources officer, or lawyer if more information is needed to assess the request.
- Be flexible and creative when considering and developing options.
- Discuss options with the person who needs accommodation.
- Take reasonable steps to accommodate the person seeking accommodation to the point of undue hardship. If full accommodation is not possible without undue hardship, try to suggest options that may partially meet the needs of the person seeking accommodation.
- Reply to the request for accommodation within a reasonable period of time.
- Make a formal agreement with the person seeking accommodation, preferably in writing, and ensure that the accommodation is given a fair opportunity to work.
- Follow up to ensure that the accommodation meets the needs of the person seeking accommodation.
- Provide details that justify a refusal to accommodate, if accommodation is not possible because it poses undue hardship or because of a bona fide occupational requirement.
- Be willing to review and modify the accommodation agreement if circumstances or needs change and the agreement is no longer working.

What are the Potential Consequences of Failing to Accommodate?

If the employer fails to provide accommodation to the point of undue hardship, then the employer may be in contravention of the *Human Rights, Citizenship and Multiculturalism Act*, and the person seeking accommodation may file a complaint with the Human Rights and Citizenship Commission. If, on the other hand, the person seeking accommodation refuses a reasonable and appropriate accommodation, the employer has likely met their legal burden.

Duty to Accommodate in Employment

The duty to accommodate in employment refers to an employer's obligation to take appropriate steps to eliminate discrimination against employees and potential employees. Discrimination may result from a rule, practice or barrier that has a negative effect on a person with a need for accommodation based on the protected grounds. An employer's duty to accommodate employees or potential employees is far reaching. It can begin when a job is first advertised and finish when the employee requiring accommodation leaves the job.

Some things to consider when accommodating employees include:

- purchasing or modifying tools, equipment or aids, as necessary,
- altering the premises to make them accessible,
- altering aspects of the job, such as job duties,
- offering flexible work schedules,
- offering rehabilitation programs,
- allowing time off for recuperation,
- transferring employees to different jobs,
- hiring an assistant,
- using temporary employees and
- adjusting policies.

Bona fide Occupational Requirement

The law recognizes that, in certain circumstances, a limitation on individual rights may be reasonable and justifiable.[1] Discrimination or exclusion may be allowed if an employer can show that a discriminatory standard, policy or rule is a necessary requirement of a job. For example, in order to perform their jobs safely, persons employed as drivers require acceptable vision and an appropriate driver's licence. A legally blind person would be legitimately excluded from a position as a driver since it is a bona fide occupational requirement to be able to see and to obtain an operator's licence.

An employer can claim a bona fide occupational requirement as a defence if a complaint of discrimination is filed against them. The onus is on the employer to show that it would be impossible to accommodate the employee without undue hardship.

The Meiorin test helps employers determine if particular occupational requirements are reasonable and justifiable. In 1999, the Supreme Court of Canada released a decision that provides direction to employers as to whether a particular occupational requirement is reasonable and justifiable. The Government of British Columbia had brought in minimum fitness standards that applied to forest firefighters. A female firefighter did not meet the requirements of a running test designed to measure aerobic fitness. Consequently, even though she had worked as a forest firefighter for three years, her employment was terminated. In grieving her dismissal, the firefighter argued that the aerobic standard discriminated against women because women generally have lower aerobic capacity than men.

In its decision, the Supreme Court outlined a new three-part test. The Meiorin test, named after the female firefighter, sets out an analysis for determining if an occupational requirement is justified. Once the complainant has shown the standard or requirement is prima facie (at first view) discriminatory, the employer must prove that, on a balance of probabilities, the standard:

- was adopted for a purpose that is rationally connected to job performance
- was adopted in an honest and good faith belief that the standard is necessary for the fulfillment of that legitimate purpose
- is necessary for the fulfillment of that legitimate purpose is reasonably necessary to accomplish that legitimate purpose—This requires the employer to demonstrate that it is impossible to accommodate the employee without the employer suffering undue hardship.

The test requires employers to accommodate or consider the capabilities of different members of society before adopting a bona fide occupational requirement. For example, women typically have lower aerobic capacity than men. Before setting a fitness standard so high that the vast majority of women would not be able to achieve it, an employer must be certain that such a high level of fitness is necessary to do the job. This does not mean that the employer cannot set standards, but it does mean that the standards should reflect the requirements of the job.

Evaluation of a bona fide Occupational Requirement

To determine whether a policy or standard is discriminatory, the Commission will first ask:

- Has the person making the complaint been treated in a differential manner?
- Is the differential treatment based on a prohibited ground?

If the answer to both questions is yes, then a prima facie case of discrimination is established. It is the responsibility of the employer to provide evidence that the standard or policy is a bona fide occupational requirement.

In order for a defence of an occupational requirement to be accepted as valid, the employer must prove that the requirement has all three characteristics described in the Meiorin test. The Commission will normally consider the following criteria for each characteristic.

Rational Connection to the Performance of the Job

- What is the purpose of the policy or standard—safety, efficiency, other? Evidence may include public statements or documents and internal documents that provide information about the work.
- What are the objective requirements of the job? Evidence may involve identifying the jobs to which the policy or standard applies and identifying the duties involved in these jobs.
- Is there a rational connection between the general purpose of the policy or standard and the objective requirements of the job?

Honest and Good Faith Belief that the Standard is Necessary

- What are the circumstances surrounding the adoption of the policy or standard?
- When was the policy or standard created by whom, and why?
- What other considerations were included in the development of the policy or standard?

Reasonable Necessity

- Was the standard or policy based on assumptions about a particular group?
- Is there evidence that the standard or policy treats a particular group

- More harshly than another without apparent justification?
- Were alternate approaches considered before the standard or policy was adopted?
- Is there any evidence the policy or standard was designed to minimize the burden on those required to comply?
- Is there accommodation to the point of undue hardship?
- Is it necessary for all employees to meet the standard or comply with the policy for the employer to accomplish its legitimate purpose?
- Is there any evidence that the legitimate purpose could be accomplished through a less discriminatory approach?

An employer who makes a successful defence based on the Meiorin test in one instance may not necessarily be able to rely on the defence in similar future situations.

Employee Privacy

While the person seeking accommodation has a right to privacy, the employer has a right to, and a need for, information that can help determine appropriate accommodation measures. The privacy issue most often arises when an employee with a disability requests accommodation from an employer.

Employers seeking medical information about an employee with a disability are not automatically entitled to a diagnosis of the employee's illness or disability or to information about the employee's specific medical treatment. Employers may request information about:
- the prognosis for full or partial recovery
- the employee's fitness to return to work
- the employee's fitness to perform specific components of the pre-injury job
- the likely duration of any physical or mental restrictions or limitations following the employee's return to work.

It is the employee's responsibility to provide information that will help the employer assess an accommodation request.

Do Changes to an Employee's Duties Affect Rate of Pay?

An employee should continue to receive the same rate of pay they received before the accommodation, unless:

- their duties have changed significantly or

- the employer would experience undue hardship to maintain their rate of pay.

Employment-related Questions about the Duty to Accommodate

Physical Disability

Q. An employee of a large moving company has developed seizures as a result of a car accident. His doctor has diagnosed mild epilepsy and has recommended that the employee take at least one month of leave from work to stabilize on medication. The employee has heard the owner of the company expressing negative views about employing people who have seizures. The employee is concerned that he will be laid off or fired. Can the employer lay off the employee because the employee has epilepsy?

A. Epilepsy is a physical disability. Physical disability is a protected ground under the *Act*. If the employee requests time off work, the employer must try to accommodate him to the point of undue hardship. The employer should not make decisions about the employee's future capabilities based on assumptions about epilepsy or on stereotypic views of persons with epilepsy. Initially, the employer could accommodate the employee by agreeing to the recommended time off. If the employer feels that the employee's absence will cause undue hardship by interfering with operations, the onus is on the employer to prove undue hardship. Options such as having other employees work more hours with overtime pay or hiring a temporary employee could be considered.

Until the requested time off has passed and the employee has returned to work, the employer should not assume that the employee will need further accommodation. If the employee returns to work with restrictions or limitations, the employer and employee need to discuss further accommodation requests.

Q. Following a heart attack, an employee of a small business asked her employer to install a stair lift because she was no longer able to climb the stairs that join the three floors on the business premises. The employer feels that she should not have to accommodate the employee because of the small size of the business. Does the employer have a duty to accommodate the employee?

A. Every employer, large or small, must make real efforts to accommodate to the point of undue hardship. Even though a business is small, it may have the financial or other resources to accommodate an individual's needs. In some cases, the costs of accommodating an employee are not significant when compared with offsetting costs such as hiring and training a new employee. Ensuring access for other employees and clients with mobility problems may also pay dividends to the company by increasing staff retention and business.

Mental Disability

Q. Following his return to work after a stress leave, an employee was dismissed. The employer indicated dissatisfaction with the employee's performance as the reason for dismissal. Can the employer dismiss the employee?

A. There must be evidence that the dismissal was based on reasons other than mental disability, such as unsatisfactory work performance that is unrelated to the disability. Such evidence could take the form of written job performance evaluations or documents outlining previous performance discussions with the employee. Any consideration of the stress leave or mental disability in the dismissal would be a violation of human rights law.

Conclusion

Accommodation is everyone's business. In order for the accommodation process to work effectively, individuals seeking accommodation and employers or service providers must work together. Effective accommodation is most often the result of good communication, creativity and flexibility. While the accommodation process may involve challenges and costs, it helps to create an inclusive society that respects diversity and human rights.

ENDNOTES

[1] *British Columbia (Public Service Employee Relations Commission) v. British Columbia Government and Service Employees' Union (B.C.G.S.E.U.)* (1999) 35 C.H.R.R. D/257 (S.C.C.)

See also *British Columbia (Superintendent of Motor Vehicles) v. British Columbia (Council of Human Rights)* (2000) 36 C.H.R.R. D/129 (S.C.C)

♦

CANADIAN HUMAN RIGHTS COMMISSION

ALCOHOL AND DRUG TESTING (2002)

Introduction

The Commission recognizes that inappropriate use of alcohol or drugs can have serious adverse effects on a person's health, safety and job performance. Safety is a prime consideration for employees and employers; however the need to ensure safety must be balanced against the requirement that employees not be discriminated against on the basis of a prohibited ground of discrimination. Workplace rules and standards that have no demonstrable relationship to job safety and performance have been found to be in violation of an employee's human rights.

In the Commission's view, drug testing is generally not acceptable, because it does not assess the effect of drug use on performance. Available drug tests do not measure impairment, how much was used or when it was used. They can only accurately determine past drug exposure. Therefore, a drug test is not a reliable means of determining whether a person is — or is not — capable of performing the essential requirements or duties of their position. That said, alcohol testing may be acceptable in some cases, because a properly administered breathalyser is a minimally intrusive and accurate measure of both consumption of alcohol and actual impairment.

If impairment is a concern in the workplace, whether from stress and anxiety, fatigue or substance abuse, an employer should focus on ways of identifying potential safety risks and remedying them, rather than taking a punitive approach to this issue. Awareness, education, effective interventions and rehabilitation are the most effective ways of ensuring that performance issues associated with alcohol and drug use are detected and resolved. An employer should consider adopting comprehensive workplace health policies that may include employee assistance programs, drug education and health promotion programs, off-site counselling and referral services, peer or supervisor monitoring.

Policy Objective

The object of this policy is to set out the Commission's interpretation of the human rights limits on drug- and alcohol-testing programs, as well as provide practical guidance on compliance with the Canadian Human Rights Act. This policy was developed following a public consultation and after studying Canadian human rights law. The Commission will apply its policies in the enforcement and interpretation of the Act.

This policy is not a substitute for legal advice and any employer considering a drug- and alcohol-testing policy should seek legal guidance on this issue.

General Policy Statement

Requiring an employee or applicant of employment to undergo a drug test as a condition of employment will, in most cases, be considered a discriminatory practice on the ground of disability. Individuals who believe they have been treated unfavourably, lose or are denied employment as a result of testing positively for past drug use, may file a complaint under the *Canadian Human Rights Act.*

Given that alcohol testing can measure impairment, alcohol testing of employees in safety-sensitive positions may be acceptable, although the employer must accommodate the needs of those who test positive.

Guiding Principles

Legal Framework

Recent decisions of the Supreme Court of Canada[1] and the Ontario Court of Appeal[2] have put into question whether drug testing, such as pre-employment and random testing, even for employees in safety-sensitive positions,[3] can ever be justified. These decisions were, in part, the impetus for the Commission's decision to update its policy on drug testing and to provide a framework for the issue of alcohol testing in the workplace.

The *Canadian Human Rights Act* prohibits discrimination on the basis of disability and perceived disability. Disability includes those with a previous or existing dependence on alcohol or a drug. Perceived disability may include an employer's perception that a person's use of alcohol or drugs makes him or her unfit to work.

In accordance with current case law on the issue of drug and alcohol testing,[4] and consistent with the Act's prohibition of discrimination on the ground of real or perceived disability, drug- and alcohol-testing policies are *prima facie* discriminatory — not only against drug-and alcohol-dependent persons, but also against all drug and alcohol users who are subject to adverse consequences as a result of detection of such use. Under the *Canadian Human Rights Act*, the issue is not whether an individual is a dependent or casual drug or alcohol user, but rather how such a person is treated by the employer. For example, testing programs may be used to deny employment to those who test positive, label a person as drug- or alcohol-dependent and impose employment conditions on those persons. Even when programs are rehabilitative in nature, such programs negatively affect employment opportunities, thus triggering the protection of the Act.

The *bona fide* occupational requirement (BFOR) is the most common defence raised by employers against allegations of employment discrimination. In the *Meiorin*[5] case, the Supreme Court of Canada set out a new test for determining whether an employer has established a BFOR and satisfied the duty of accommodation short of undue hardship. Under the test, the following questions must be asked:

1. Did the employer adopt the policy or standard for a purpose rationally connected to the performance of the job?
2. Did the employer adopt the particular policy or standard in an honest and good faith belief that it was necessary to the fulfilment of that legitimate, work-related purpose?
3. Is the policy or standard reasonably necessary to the accomplishment of that legitimate, work-related purpose?

This last element requires the employer to show that the policy or standard adopted is the least discriminatory way to achieve the purpose or goal in relation to the particular jobs to which the policy or standard applies. It includes the requirement for the employer to demonstrate that it is impossible to accommodate individual employees without imposing undue hardship. (See section on Accommodation and Undue Hardship.)

As a result of the *Meiorin* decision, the Commission has modified its approach to the investigation of complaints related to employment standards. All allegedly discriminatory standards and policies must be justified as rationally connected to the work or service, made in good faith, and reasonably necessary. Investigations now also consider whether the standard has the effect of excluding on impressionistic assumptions members of a particular group, or treating one or more groups more harshly than others without apparent justification. The onus is on the respondent (i.e. the employer) to provide evidence of each of the elements of the test set out by the Court.

Legal Decisions on Alcohol and Drug Testing

In *Entrop v. Imperial Oil,*[6] the Ontario Court of Appeal had an opportunity to apply the *Meiorin* test to the issue of drug and alcohol testing. The case involved an employee of Imperial Oil who was compelled under company policy to reveal a past drinking problem. The employee, Martin Entrop, was subsequently removed from his position in a "safety-sensitive" area, despite the fact that he had been alcohol-free for several years. Mr. Entrop then filed a complaint with the Ontario Human Rights Commission. His complaint triggered an analysis of drug- and alcohol-testing policies in the workplace that went all the way to the Ontario Court of Appeal.

First, the Court of Appeal concluded that alcohol and drug testing is *prima facie* discriminatory. It then applied the test developed by the Supreme Court in *Meiorin* to determine whether, and in what circumstances, drug and alcohol tests may be justified as bona fide occupational requirements. The Court concluded that Imperial Oil had satisfied the first two steps of the test set out by the Supreme Court: rational connection and honest and good faith belief.

In considering the third branch of the test, the Court first noted a critical difference between alcohol and drug tests. Alcohol tests, i.e. a breathalyser, can test whether a person is actually impaired at the moment the test is administered. That is, an alcohol test, if applied to a person on the job, can tell whether that person is fit to do his or her job. On the other hand, the Court noted drug tests, such as urinalysis, cannot measure whether a person is under the effect of a drug at the time the test is administered. A drug test can only detect past drug use. An employer who administers a drug test cannot tell whether that person is impaired at the moment, nor whether they are likely to be impaired while on the job.

With this distinction established, the Court considered alcohol or drug tests in various circumstances. For example, the Court concluded that random alcohol testing of employees was permissible for employees in safety-sensitive positions. In the opinion of the Court, employers can legitimately take steps to detect alcohol impairment among its employees in safety-sensitive positions, where supervision is limited or non-existent.

In his comments on drug testing, Justice Laskin reasoned that, because drug testing cannot measure present impairment, future impairment or likely impairment on the job, Imperial Oil could not justify pre-employment testing or random drug testing for employees in safety-sensitive (or other) positions as reasonably necessary to accomplish Imperial Oil's legitimate goal of a safe workplace, free from impairment (the third branch of the Supreme Court test). Further, the Ontario Court of Appeal found drug-testing programs had not been shown to be effective in reducing drug use, work accidents or work performance problems.

The Court held that drug testing for "reasonable cause" or "post-accident" and post-reinstatement, may be acceptable if "...necessary as one facet of a larger process of assessment of drug abuse." Neither the tribunal nor the courts elaborated on what larger process of assessment is required.

The Court also concluded that Imperial Oil's sanction for a positive test by an employee in a safety- sensitive position — dismissal — was not sufficiently sensitive to individual capabilities.

Based on this decision, it would appear that if an employer seeks to introduce random drug testing into the workplace, it will only be successful if there is drug-testing technology that can demonstrate a current state of impairment, as a breathalyser can demonstrate alcohol impairment.

The *Entrop* decision is final and will not be appealed. It will bind arbitrators and tribunals in Ontario in the future, and will be highly persuasive in proceedings in other provinces and territories.

Application

Pre-employment Drug and Alcohol Testing

Testing for alcohol or drugs is a form of medical examination. Any employment related medical examination or inquiry must be limited to determining an individual's ability to perform the essential duties of the job. An employer must therefore demonstrate that pre-employment drug and alcohol testing provides an effective assessment of an applicant's ability to discharge their employment responsibilities. Since a positive pre-employment drug or alcohol test will in no way predict whether the individual will be impaired at any time while on the job, pre-employment testing cannot be shown to be reasonably necessary to accomplish the legitimate goal of hiring non-impaired workers. Pre-employment drug and alcohol testing fails the "reasonable necessity" arm of the Meoirin test and is contrary to the Act.

It is also the Commission's position that conducting automatic drug and alcohol tests as part of a medical assessment for certification contravenes the spirit of the *Canadian Human Rights Act*. Testing as a pre-condition or certification for employment in a safety-sensitive position should only occur in limited circumstances, such as where the individual has disclosed an existing or past drug abuse problem or where a general medical exam provides reasonable cause to believe that an individual may become impaired while on the job.

Random Testing for Drugs and Alcohol

Random drug testing, whether an employee holds a safety-sensitive position or not, is contrary to the *Canadian Human Rights Act*, because it fails the "reasonable necessity" test. Since a positive drug test cannot measure present impairment and can only confirm that a person has been exposed to drugs at some point in the past (sometimes as much as several weeks in the past), it cannot identify whether a person was impaired while on the job. Random drug tests therefore cannot be shown to be reasonably necessary to accomplish the goal of ensuring that workers are not impaired by drugs.

As long as employees are notified that alcohol testing is a condition of employment, random alcohol testing of employees in safety-sensitive positions may be permissible, although the employer must meet the duty to accommodate the needs of those who test positive. Random alcohol testing can pass the *Meiorin* test, where random drug testing does not, because a breathalyser reading can identify whether or not a person is impaired while on the job.

Random alcohol testing of an employee in a non-safety-sensitive position is not acceptable. Unless an employer has reasonable cause to believe the employee is unfit to do his or her job as a result of alcohol use (addressed below), an employer cannot demonstrate that it is reasonably necessary to administer breathalyser tests to ensure effective job performance.

Given that the focus is on testing for impairment of one's ability to perform the essential duties of a position, zero tolerance for alcohol no matter when consumed will generally be considered unnecessarily strict.

"Reasonable Cause" and "Post-Incident" Drug and Alcohol Testing

"Reasonable cause" or "post-incident" testing, for either alcohol or drugs, in a safety-sensitive environment may be acceptable in specific circumstances. For example, where an employee reports to work in an unfit condition and there are reasonable grounds to believe there is an underlying problem of substance abuse, or following an accident, a near miss or report of dangerous behaviour, an employer will have a legitimate interest in assessing whether an employee has used substances that may have contributed to the incident. An employer can generally establish that "reasonable cause" and "post-incident" testing is reasonably necessary to ensure the heightened safety standard that is necessary in risk-sensitive environments, if testing is part of a broader program of medical assessment, monitoring and support.

"Reasonable cause" and "post-incident" testing, if justified, should be conducted as soon as reasonably practical, but not where there is evidence that the act or omission of the employee could not have been a contributing factor to the accident (e.g. structural or mechanical failure).

In rare cases, dismissal or permanent re-assignment will be warranted for a positive test result but, in reaching such a decision, employers must bear in mind the general rule of individualized consideration to the point of undue hardship.

"Reasonable cause" and "post-incident" drug and alcohol testing of employees in non-safety-sensitive positions has not been an issue that has come before the courts. It may be that an employer could establish such testing was a BFOR, if it were successful in meeting the "reasonable necessity" arm of the *Meiorin* test. That is, an employer would have to show that, in a particular employee's case, the circumstances were such that no other means were possible, short of undue hardship to the employer, to ensure the accomplishment of a legitimate objective such as workplace safety. For office workers in regular contact with co-workers and supervisors, proving such a case would be difficult, but not inconceivable. Testing should only be considered if an employee's on-the-job behaviour provides reasonable grounds to believe he or she is impaired by drugs or alcohol.

Mandatory Disclosure

In *Entrop*, the Ontario Court of Appeal accepted that an employer could impose a work rule that requires employees working in a safety-sensitive position to disclose current substance abuse problems, as well past problems with alcohol or drugs (within the last 5 or 6 years for alcohol dependancy and 6 years for drug dependency, the point where the risk of relapse is "no greater than the risk a member of the general population will suffer a substance abuse problem.")

Automatic dismissal or refusal to employ an individual based on a disclosure of past or present dependency on drugs or alcohol is not in keeping with the requirement by the employer under the *Canadian Human Rights Act* to provide accommodation to the point of undue hardship. Failure to disclose an alcohol or drug problem should also not be grounds for dismissal as denial is a symptom of addiction.

Generally, employees in non-safety-sensitive positions need not disclose past dependency on alcohol or drugs unless an employer can establish that such a disclosure is a BFOR. The duty to accommodate, including individualized assistance and consideration, will apply.

Follow-Up Testing

Unannounced periodic or random testing may be permissible, following disclosure of a current drug or alcohol dependency or abuse problem, as long as it is tailored to individual circumstances and is part of a broader program of monitoring, rehabilitation and support. Usually, the designated rehabilitation provider will determine whether follow-up testing is necessary for a particular individual.

Fitness-for-Duty Testing

The Commission supports the use of functional performance testing, where such methods exist, to assess impairment. When minimally intrusive, reliable tests of impairment capable of giving an accurate and meaningful result generally become available, it might be feasible and acceptable to test safety sensitive employees for impairment — whether from drugs, alcohol, anxiety, and stress or fatigue. If standardized tests are employed, care must be taken to ensure that testing methods do not have any inherent biases, for example against women or visible minorities.

Cross-Border Trucking and Bus Operations: A Special Case

Canadian trucking and bus companies wishing to do business in the U.S. may be required to develop drug- and alcohol-testing programs to comply with U.S. regulations. Nevertheless, these programs must respect Canadian human rights law.

Canadian human rights law takes a different approach to the U.S. on the issue drug testing — not because protecting the rights of those who abuse drugs or alcohol is considered more important than public safety, but because drug testing has not been shown to be effective in reducing drug use, work accidents or work performance problems.

However, for trucking and bus businesses that operate exclusively or predominantly between Canada and the U.S., not being banned from driving in the U.S. may be a bona fide occupational requirement, provided the company can produce evidence that its continued employment of banned drivers would constitute an undue hardship.

Drivers who are denied employment opportunities or who face disciplinary or other discriminatory employment consequences in Canada as a result of the imposition of the U.S. rules will still have a right to file a complaint with the Canadian Human Rights Commission on the ground of real or perceived disability.

Drivers who, on the basis of individualized assessment, have been proven to be substance-dependent, must be accommodated by their employer in accordance with Canadian law and jurisprudence.

Upon successful completion of evaluation, treatment and rehabilitation, drivers may be considered for appropriate employment, including reassignment to Canada-only routes, unless doing so would constitute an undue hardship.

If a driver tests positive for drugs or alcohol and is determined not to be substance-dependent, the driver should be returned to his or her position, if possible, and appropriate disciplinary action may be taken. Termination may only be justified where there is just cause and appropriate disciplinary steps have been taken.

Policy Requirements

Accommodation

In the limited circumstances in which testing is justified, employees who test positive must be accommodated by the employer to the point of undue hardship. The Act requires individualized or personalized accommodation measures. Policies that result in automatic loss of employment, reassignment, or that impose inflexible reinstatement conditions without regard for personal circumstances are unlikely to meet this requirement. Accommodation should include referring the employee to a substance abuse professional to determine if in fact he or she is drug-dependent, providing the necessary support to permit the employee to undergo treatment or a rehabilitation program, and considering sanctions less severe than dismissal.

An employer may be justified in temporarily removing an employee with an active or recently active substance abuse problem from a safety-sensitive position. Automatic reassignment is not acceptable.

Once rehabilitation has been successfully completed, the employee should be returned to his or her position. Follow-up testing may be a condition of continued employment where safety continues to be of fundamental importance. Usually, the designated rehabilitation provider will determine whether follow-up testing is necessary for a particular individual. If follow-up testing reveals continuing drug or alcohol use, further employer action, up to dismissal, may be justified.

If the employee is determined *not* to be substance-dependent, the employee should be returned to his or her position and appropriate disciplinary action may be taken. Appropriate consequences for a breach of an employer's drug or alcohol testing policy depend on the facts of the case, including: the nature of the violation, the existence of prior infractions, the response to prior corrective programs, and the seriousness of the violation.

An employee that requests assistance for an alcohol or drug problem cannot be disciplined for seeking help.

Undue Hardship

The employer will be relieved of the duty to accommodate the individual needs of the alcohol or drug dependent employee if the employer can show that:

1. the cost of accommodation would alter the nature or affect the viability of the enterprise, OR
2. notwithstanding the accommodation efforts, health or safety risks to workers or members of the public are so serious that they outweigh the benefits of providing equal treatment to the worker with an addiction or dependency.

If an employee has problem with drugs or alcohol and it is interfering with that person's ability to perform the essential duties of the job, the employer must provide the support necessary to enable that person to undertake a rehabilitation program, unless the employer can demonstrate that such accommodation would cause undue hardship.

If an employer has reasonable cause to believe an employee is abusing drugs or alcohol or an employee tests positive and refuses treatment, this does not in and of itself constitute undue hardship or justify immediate dismissal of the individual. The employer must demonstrate through progressive discipline that the employee has been warned and is unable to perform the essential requirements of his or her position.

Ensuring Compliance

In addition to the many factors discussed in this policy, the Commission may also consider some of the following elements when reviewing a drug- or alcohol-testing policy.

In the limited circumstances where drug or alcohol testing may be considered a valid requirement of the job:

- Does the employer notify applicants of this requirement at the time that an offer of employment is made? The circumstances under which testing may be required should be made clear to employees and applicants.
- Are drug- or alcohol-testing samples collected by accredited individuals and are the results analysed by a certified laboratory?
- Are procedures in place to ensure that a health care professional reviews the test results with the employee or applicant concerned? All confirmed positive results should be evaluated to determine if there is an explanation for the positive result other than substance abuse. An affected individual or employee should have the right to submit a request to have their sample re-tested by an accredited laboratory should the original results be in dispute.

- Are procedures in place to ensure confidentiality of test results? Any records concerning drug and alcohol tests should be kept in a separate confidential file away from other employee records.

There are many causes of employee impairment besides alcohol and drug use that jeopardize workplace safety, such as fatigue, stress, anxiety and personal problems. The Commission encourages employers to adopt programs and policies that focus on methods of detection of impairment and safety risks, and that are remedial rather than punitive in nature. These would include employee assistance programs, enhanced supervision and observation, and positive peer reporting systems, which focus on rehabilitation rather than punishment. Testing should be limited to determining actual impairment of an employee's ability to perform or fulfill the essential duties or requirements of the job.

ENDNOTES

[1] *British Columbia (Public ServiceEmployee Relations Comm.) v. British Columbia Government and Service Employees' Union*, [1999] 3 S.C.R. 3, also referred to as the Meiorin case.

[2] *Entrop v. Imperial Oil* (2000), 50 O.R. (3d) 18 (Ont. C.A.)

[3] A safety-sensitive job is one in which incapacity due to drug or alcohol impairment could result in direct and significant risk of injury to the employee, others or the environment. Whether a job can be categorized as safety-sensitive must be considered within the context of the industry, the particular workplace and an employee's direct involvement in a high risk operation. Any definition must take into account the role of properly trained supervisors and the checks and balances present in the workplace.

[4] *Entrop v. Imperial Oil* (2000), 50 O.R. (3d) 18 (Ont. C.A.)

[5] *British Columbia (Public ServiceEmployee Relations Comm.) v. British Columbia Government and Service Employees' Union*, [1999] 3 S.C.R. 3

[6] (2000), 50 O.R. (3d) 18 (Ont. C.A.)

◆
NEW BRUNSWICK HUMAN RIGHTS COMMISSION

DRUG AND ALCOHOL TESTING (DRAFT)

Introduction

The Commission recognises the importance of maintaining a safe workplace. However the need to ensure safety must be balanced against the requirement that employees be treated equally. Workplace policies that have no demonstrable relationship to job safety and performance have at times been found to be in violation of an employee's human rights.

One method implemented by employers in order to ensure a safe work environment is alcohol and drug testing. These tests are sometimes imposed before and during employment and they can affect a minority of workers or all the workers in an organization. Since more and more organisations are using this method, which is a threat to privacy and freedom from discrimination for the disabled, the Commission believes it is time to examine its conformity with human rights law. Furthermore, the Commission wants to highlight the fact that notwithstanding that this method is quite prevalent in North America, particularly in the United States, employers who use it in New Brunswick must respect the *Code*.

This guideline seeks to clarify the rights and responsibilities of job applicants, employees and employers, with respect to employment-related drug and alcohol testing. The Guideline will also clarify the Commission's interpretation of the *Code* in its compliance function. Commission staff may therefore make reference to the guidelines in the exercise of their functions in application of the *Code*. Commission staff will also be guided by other more general principles of interpretation in the application of the *Code*.

Dependence on Drugs or Alcohol is a Disability

Discrimination on the basis of physical disability or mental disability, with respect to all aspects of employment be it the hiring process, employment agencies, or the operation of trade unions and employers' organisations, is prohibited under s.3 of the *Code*. Specifically, section 3(1), which applies to the employer in particular, provides that:

3(1) No employer, employer's organisation or other person acting on the behalf of an employer shall

   (a) refuse to employ or continue to employ any person, or
   (b) discriminate against any person in respect of employment or any term or condition of employment,

because of race, colour, religion, national origin, ancestry, place of origin, age, physical disability, mental disability, marital status, sexual orientation or sex.

Section 2 defines "physical disability" as:

   any degree of disability, infirmity, malformation or disfigurement of a physical nature caused by bodily injury, illness or birth defects and, without limiting the generality of the foregoing, includes any disability resulting from any degree of paralysis or from diabetes mellitus, epilepsy, amputation, lack of physical co-ordination, blindness or visual impediment, muteness or speech impediment, or physical reliance on a guide dog or on a wheelchair, cane, crutch or other remedial device or appliance;

Section 2 defines "mental disability" as:

   (a) any condition of mental retardation or impairment,
   (b) any learning disability, or dysfunction in one or more of the mental processes involved in the comprehension or use of symbols or spoken language, or
   (c) any mental disorder;

A dependence on alcohol or drugs is a disability because it is an illness that creates physical disability, mental impairment or mental disorder and interferes with physical, psychological and social functioning.[1]

Prior Alcohol or Drug Dependence — The Perception of a Disability

If you have had a prior alcohol or drug dependency you will be protected by the *Code* under the grounds of physical disability and mental disability. The Commission considers that any action towards an individual based on the belief that a prior dependency creates a disability is discrimination based on the perception of a disability. Such discrimination, therefore, is prohibited under the *Code* on the grounds of physical disability and mental disability. An employment policy that will likely discriminate in this way will be considered a violation of the *Code*.[2] It is worth noting that the perception of disability is not solely about prior dependence. For example, if individuals are perceived as having an addiction to drugs or alcohol, even though they do not and never have, the *Code* will protect them as well. In the same way, the *Code* will protect a person with no addiction who uses drugs or alcohol occasionally.

Example

Cheryl enjoyed working for her company. She had made close friends of several of her co-workers and they liked to eat together and talk in the lunchroom during breaks. During one of these breaks, Cheryl revealed that she had been through a drug treatment program and was now very happy with her new life. However, her supervisor overheard that conversation and reported it to the administration. In response, the company announced that it was implementing random drug testing beginning in Cheryl's department, even though it was not a safety sensitive area. Of course, the first candidate for their random testing was Cheryl. After encouragement by friends and family, Cheryl called the Human Rights Commission to file a complaint against her employers.

The Employment Application

In the past, as an employer you may have screened out applicants with prior or existing drug or alcohol dependencies based on medical information gained through pre-employment medical examinations or questions. These methods of gathering information, which function as part of the application screening process, are now prohibited by s. 3(4) of the *Code*.

Your pre-employment evaluation should be limited to determining an individual's ability to perform the essential duties of a job. A positive pre-employment drug or alcohol test does not predict whether the individual will be impaired while on duty, and is therefore considered an unnecessary discriminatory practice.

Pre-employment drug or alcohol testing may take place after a conditional offer of employment in a safety sensitive position is made in limited circumstances, such as where the individual has disclosed an existing or past abuse problem or where a general medical exam provides reasonable cause to believe that an individual may become impaired on the job. A safety sensitive position is one in which incapacity due to drug or alcohol impairment could result in direct and significant risk of injury to others or of damage to the environment. The conditional offer of employment should be written, not verbal.[3] The circumstances under which such testing might be required should be made clear to the applicant. Keeping the selection process free from medical questions and testing ensures that an applicant with any type of disability is considered exclusively on her or his merits.

Example

After researching mining companies across Canada, Kevin responded to a listing for an elevator operator with Silver Mines Inc. The ad stated that the elevator operator would be responsible for bringing employees to and from work. It also stated that the elevator shaft reached a depth of up to 20 floors under ground and is considered a safety sensitive position. During his first interview with Silver Mines Inc., Kevin was informed that, should he be short-listed, he would only be offered a position if he tested negative in a mandatory drug test. Kevin wanted the job, so he signed the conditional agreement, but after considering the invasion of privacy he questioned the validity of the drug testing. After some telephone calls, Kevin was informed by the Human Rights Commission, that in order for the company to legally administer the drug test, they would need a valid reason for implementing it. Since Kevin did not have any previous drug history, or any condition, medical or otherwise, that would indicate he posed a safety risk, there was no valid reason for the company to impose a drug test. Subsequently, Kevin was offered the position without the "mandatory drug test".

The Personal Interview

The *Code* prohibits oral or written questions that express preferences of the employer or require a job applicant to divulge information respecting any of the prohibited grounds listed in s. 3(3). As previously stated, drug and alcohol dependencies are protected within the grounds of physical disability and mental disability that are listed in s. 3(3). Notwithstanding this prohibition, mandatory disclosure of present dependency as well as past problems with drugs or alcohol within the last 6 years may be permissible for employees holding safety-sensitive positions.

Example

Kate was a single mother of three who had experienced a nervous breakdown in her past. The breakdown had been exacerbated by a drug dependency. Fortunately, Kate was treated for both conditions successfully. A few years later, she finished law school with an excellent GPA. Kate was pleased when she secured an interview with the prestigious law firm, Best & Choice. However, as the interview progressed, Kate began to feel frustrated. Instead of discussing her professional qualifications, she was asked if she had ever had trouble with drug and alcohol dependency or mental illness. Kate answered the questions honestly, doing her best to emphasize her successful recovery, present health and professional qualifications. However, although the panel of interviewers did not audibly express their concerns and apprehensions regarding Kate's past, by the end of the interview it was obvious that Best & Choice was not interested in her as a prospective employee. In response to encouragement from her friends and family, Kate filed a complaint against Best & Choice with the Human Rights Commission.

Testing Policies

In the event of a complaint concerning a drug or alcohol testing policy that intends to aid in the removal, demotion, etc. of individuals who use alcohol or drugs, the Commission will consider the policy to be, on the face of it, discriminatory.(4) The question the Commission will ask, in the event of a complaint concerning such a policy, is whether the policy is a *bona fide* occupational qualification (BFOQ). That is to say that the policy is genuinely connected to determining whether the job applicants or employees are able to meet the essential job requirements and that there is no reasonable alternative to the policy that is less discriminatory.(5) The most well known alternatives are: employee assistance programs, peer monitoring, supervisory reviews, health promotion programs, referral services, off-site counseling and functional performance testing.

Example

"Silver Summer" is a resort that caters to horse lovers, offering promotional packages that include overnight trail rides etc. Recently, the administrative staff was concerned to find that some of its employees were involved to varying degrees with illicit drugs. As an alternative to termination, and as an expression of the value placed on their employees, Silver Summer implemented a Drug Prevention Program. The resort contracted lecturers and addictions counselors to run a compulsory weeklong workshop, however, the follow-up program was excellent. It consisted of group support meetings for addictions that were offered on a permanent basis at 12 different times during the week. The results of this program were impressive. Silver Summer recognized that they had made the best choice for their employees and for the economic health of their company.

Drug Testing

The Court stated, in *Entrop*, that random drug testing of employees or pre-employment drug testing is a violation of human rights partly because it cannot assess actual impairment on the job, it can only detect past drug use. Drug tests should be given only where there is reasonable cause to suspect an impaired ability by the employee to satisfactorily and safely perform job duties or if an incident just happened, such as an accident that may have been a result of drug use. In addition, a drug test may be acceptable for an employee who divulged a dependency or for an employee who has reintegrated into the workplace following a rehabilitation program. In each case the drug testing must be part of a larger process of drug abuse evaluation and the employees must be notified that drug testing is a condition of employment.

Example

Elaine was delighted that she had been chosen by her company to attend an International Conference. Because it was held overseas, she was required to submit to a drug test. Elaine confidently procured her passport, underwent a compulsory medical examination, and scheduled immunizations. However, one week before she was to leave for the Conference she was called into the head office of her company. She was informed that she had tested positive for marijuana. Elaine was devastated. She had not used marijuana in several weeks and she had certainly never used illicit drugs on a workday. Since the administration considered the results of the test as a reflection of Elaine's ability to represent the company, she was not allowed to attend the conference.

In the above example, the company was in error because the testing did not adequately assess Elaine's ability to represent the company or perform her duties.

Alcohol Testing

In *Entrop*, the Court held that employees in safety sensitive positions where supervision is limited or non-existent may be randomly tested for alcohol use, because a positive breathalyser test for alcohol shows actual impairment on the job. Alcohol testing may also be acceptable in situations where there is just cause to believe an employee is drunk at work or if an incident occurs, such as an accident that may have been a result of alcohol use, or when an employee returns to the workplace after a rehabilitation program. In each case employees must be notified that alcohol testing is a condition of employment and testing must be part of a broader process of alcohol abuse evaluation. Obviously, pre-employment alcohol testing and random alcohol testing of employees in non-safety sensitive positions are prohibited at all times.

Example

Don has owned a construction company in Florida for the last twenty years. He has dealt with his share of workers who use alcohol and drugs on the job. Currently, Don uses a breathalyser for random tests on heavy equipment operators. One afternoon, water began spraying everywhere from a broken water main. Apparently the backhoe had caused the breakage. The backhoe operator appeared disoriented and red-faced after the accident. Since Don was nearby at the time, he was able to perform a breathalyser test almost immediately following the accident. The backhoe operator's alcohol blood levels were considerably above the legal limit. Don responded by suspending the operator and offering to pay for the worker to enter a local addiction treatment centre. Although the operator threatened to make a human rights complaint against Don, he decided not to follow through. He was informed by the Intake Officer at the Commission that human rights law supports breathalyser tests in safety sensitive positions, especially after a suspicious accident.

Renunciation to the Protection of the Code

It is clear that no one can renounce the right to equality in an individual contract or a collective agreement.[6]

Example

Sherrie and Louise worked for a privately run nursing home in Saint John. Apparently, the owner had some concerns about the use of drugs and alcohol by employees. During the year, each employee was served with an agreement that required a signature if they wanted to continue working at the nursing home. The agreement set a deadline, after which, the employee could be terminated without proof of signature. The agreement gave the nursing home the right to examine all medical files of employees, as well as the right to perform random drug and alcohol tests. It was also stated that should any medical files reveal past or present drug or alcohol dependency, the nursing home retained the right to terminate the individual based on this information. The agreement provided also that the employee waived any right to take action or to complain to Employment Standards or the Human Rights Commission as a result of any termination or disciplinary action flowing from a breach of agreement. Sherrie and Louise informed the owners that the contract was in contravention of human rights law. However, the owners ignored this information. Consequently, Sherrie and Louise felt compelled to complain to the Human Rights Commission.

Bona Fide Occupational Qualifications (BFOQ's)

Once the complainant has proven a *prima facie* case of discrimination the onus shifts to the respondent to raise a defense. The respondent could be an employer, or a Human Resource Officer, etc. To prove a *prima facie* case of discrimination the complainant must demonstrate that there is an existence of a factor such as random drug and alcohol testing, and that the effect results in the exclusion, restriction or preference of a group of persons who are identified by a prohibited ground of discrimination. For the purposes of this guideline, the grounds of discrimination would be physical and mental disability. Finally, membership in the protected group must be demonstrated. Basically, a *prima facie* case of discrimination is a case where on first appearance, but subject to further evidence, there is discrimination.

In some circumstances, the nature or degree of a person's disability may preclude that individual from performing the essential duties of a job. Section 3(7)(a) of the *Code* provides that a termination of employment or a refusal to employ a person because of a *bona fide* occupational qualification based on the nature of work or the circumstance of the place of work in relation to the physical disability or mental disability, as determined by the Commission, is allowable.

The standard for the proof of a BFOQ with respect to a drug and alcohol testing policy will be high. This is so because of the invasive nature of drug and alcohol testing and the serious impact that the results of the testing may have on individuals. Here again, we must highlight the difference between drug testing, which is a urine analysis and arguably a more egregious invasion of privacy, and alcohol testing, usually a breathalyser test, which is somewhat less intrusive.

Considerable empirical evidence will be required to show that the policy is necessary, that the methods used are reliable and that the drug or alcohol use discovered by the testing is linked to poor or dangerous job performance.[7]

In the event of a complaint, an employer will be obligated to prove that ithe testing provisions under its policy are necessary to determine incapability to perform the essential duties of the job to the satisfaction of the Commission. The employer's assessment must be fair and accurate.

In the event of a complaint, an employer who wishes to defend a drug or alcohol testing policy must meet the three-part test developed by the Supreme Court of Canada in *Meiorin*[8]:

1. The employer has adopted the testing policy for a purpose that is rationally connected to the performance of the job;
2. The employer has adopted the testing policy in an honest and good faith belief that it was necessary to that work-related purpose; and
3. The testing policy must be reasonably necessary to accomplish that work-related purpose. To show that the test is reasonably necessary, it must be proven that the testing policy is the least discriminatory way to achieve the work-related purpose and that it is impossible to accommodate individual employees sharing the characteristics of the complainant without imposing undue hardship upon the employer.

Please see the New Brunswick Human Rights Commission Guideline entitled *The Duty to Accommodate and BFOQ's/BFQ's* for more information on how the Commission determines whether a BFOQ exists as a defense in a particular case.

Duty to Accommodate

If an employer is able to show that a drug or alcohol testing policy is a BFOQ, then the employer will have further obligations to employees found to have drug or alcohol dependencies. The employer must attempt to accommodate an employee with a drug or alcohol dependency up to the point of undue hardship. This means the employer will generally be required to accommodate if accommodations can be made

a) without unreasonable financial expense for the employer;
b) without extreme interference with the operation of the business, such as would alter the nature of the business; and
c) without creating a significant safety risk for the returning employee, other staff or clients.

This may include taking steps in an effort to provide the employee with a chance to rehabilitate herself or himself and to return to work following a treatment program.[9] Further, the individual must be tested against a realistic standard that reflects his or her capacities and potential contributions. Therefore, accommodation may require individual assessment.[10]

The duty to accommodate extends to all facets of the employment process: hiring, employment testing, on-the-job training, working conditions, transfers, promotions, etc.

The Human Rights Board of Inquiry has very broad remedial powers. It can impose any reasonable steps deemed necessary for the employer to accommodate the complainant.

Here is a list of examples of accommodation for an employee with drug or alcohol dependency:

(1) transfer employee from safety-sensitive position to non safety-sensitive position;

(2) offer rehabilitation programs and hire a temporary employee to replace an employee absent during the program if necessary;

(3) adjust the application of employer policies with respect to job security.

Example

Pete has a high stress job. He is Director of the Hazardous Waste Unit at LMNOP Chemical Corporation. A year ago, it became known that Pete was struggling with a drug addiction. His employers supported him by allowing time off to participate in a treatment program. In the meantime, they temporarily filled his position with the promise, that when he was ready, his job would be waiting for him. Initially, Pete returned to work in a low stress office position. However, when he felt confident enough, he requested to be returned back to his previous position as Director. As promised, he was reinstated.

This is a good example of accommodation. The employers took reasonable steps to accommodate their employee's disability.

Undue Hardship

Undue hardship means there may be costs. The term implies "inconvenience, and some degree of disruption and expense." In order to be deemed undue, the hardship must outweigh the benefits of providing equal treatment to the worker.

It is the employer that bears the onus of proving that accommodation has been met or that it is impossible to accommodate the complainant due to undue hardship. Therefore, it is critical that the employer document its action in determining whether an employee can be accommodated.

The extent to which the employer is required to accommodate an employee with a drug or alcohol dependency depends on various factors, including:

(a) costs of the required accommodation;
(b) size of the operation;
(c) economic conditions facing employer;
(d) availability of other positions;
(e) health and safety concerns;[11] and,
(f) past efforts to accommodate.

Example

Fred is a long-standing employee at the local meat packing plant. It's a small operation and Fred was warned during his orientation about company safety concerns regarding the use of knives and blades and employee conduct on the plant floor. Unfortunately, Fred has an alcohol addiction problem. His employer has sent him on two clinics in the past two years. Fred has a pattern of dependency, treatment, sobriety and then dependency again. Three weeks after his return to work from a previous clinic for alcohol addiction, he showed up drunk at work and started threatening other staff with a butcher's knife. The shift foreman called security. Fred was calmed down and sent home. One of his co-workers received a deep cut to his right forearm in a scuffle that arose during the attempts to restrain Fred. Fred's termination papers followed later that day.

Duty of the Individual with a Drug or Alcohol-Related Disability

A person with an alcohol or drug dependency who requires accommodation in order to perform the essential duties of a job has a responsibility to communicate her or his needs in sufficient detail and to co-operate in consultations and treatment to enable the employer to respond to its duty to accommodate.[12] If the employee refuses to acknowledge the problem and to seek counseling when it is required, the employer may implement progressive discipline and performance management and, only if necessary, take further disciplinary steps. The employee's duty to communicate his or her needs does not interfere with the employer's obligation to treat him or her equally.

Where the employer takes reasonable steps towards accommodation and further steps would result in undue hardship, the employee may also have to take accommodating steps to mitigate his or her loss.

Example

David worked in a shipyard as a naval mechanic. He had spent years with engines and was somewhat of a genius. However his marijuana addiction had progressed to the point where he was consuming drugs every day. Because of this addiction, David's work was suffering, although he did not seem to be aware of it. His supervisor Mike, who really valued David as an employee, had spoken to him several times about showing up to work high. Eventually the employer recommended a Drug Addiction Program for David and he enrolled. After one week David stopped attending the sessions and resumed his drug use. He returned to work insisting that he was drug free and had been cured. His counselor recommended completing this three-week program and a gradual return to work with ongoing counseling. He refused to complete the program and was suspended. David brought a human rights complaint that was settled in early mediation following his undertaking to resume his drug addiction counseling.

Considerations when Developing On-the-job Testing Criteria

Employers should have regard to the following considerations when developing on-the-job testing criteria:

1. Qualified professionals must perform drug and alcohol testing and the results must be analysed in a competent laboratory.
2. All health assessment information should remain exclusively with the examining physician's files and away from the employee's personnel file.
3. Procedures should be instituted for the physician to review the test results with the employee concerned.
4. Testing should not be used to reveal anything other than drug and/or alcohol use.
5. When a test is positive, there should be a second test to confirm the result before any action is taken.
6. If a drug test on a dark skinned person reveals the presence of THC, the active substance in cannabis, the employer must be very careful before taking any further measures. This is because dark skinned persons have more melanin in their skin and hair, which produces the same reaction to the test as THC.

Summary

The New Brunswick *Human Rights Code* prohibits discrimination on the basis of disability and perceived disability. Disability includes those with a previous or existing dependence on drug or alcohol.

Because they cannot be established as BFOQ, the following types of testing are prohibited at all times:

- Pre-employment drug testing;
- Pre-employment alcohol testing;
- Random drug testing; and,
- Random alcohol testing of employees in non-safety sensitive positions.

If an employer can demonstrate that they are BFOQ, the following types of testing may be acceptable:

- Random alcohol testing of employees in safety sensitive positions;
- Drug or alcohol testing for "reasonable cause" or "post-accident"; and
- Random or periodic testing following disclosure of a current drug or alcohol dependency.

In the limited circumstances where testing is justified, employers must accommodate the employees who test positive up to the point of undue hardship.

The employer will be relieved of the duty to accommodate the individual needs of the disabled employee, if he can show that the negative effects of the accommodation on the enterprise would make it impossible.

The Commission supports the use of non-discriminatory methods for dealing with employee impairment, such as employee assistance programs, peer monitoring, supervisory reviews, health promotion programs, referral services, off-site counseling and functional performance testing.

ENDNOTES

[1]   *Entrop v. Imperial Oil* (2000) 50 O.R. 3d 18 (C.A.).

[2]   The Ontario *Human Rights Code* specifically includes previous "handicaps" and the N.B. Human Rights Act does not. However, the Commission treats discrimination based on the perception of a disability as discrimination based on a disability. Therefore, the wording in *Entrop v. Imperial Oil* (1996), 27 CH.R.R. D/212 applies in this guideline:

> The definition of 'handicap' under the *Code* includes persons who 'has had' a 'handicap'. This ensures that individuals who may have been drug users in the past, but who

no longer suffer from an on-going disability, are included within the protection of the *Code*. The language of the *Code* also ensures that complaints that allege discrimination because of past or present drug abuse problems are not required to establish that their condition actually creates a mental or physical disability. To the extent that an employer perceives that the drug use causes a disability and then acts on the basis of this perception to discriminate against employees, this also falls within the ambit of the legislative protection.

[3] *Canadian Civil Liberties Assn. v. Toronto Dominion Bank*, [1994] C.H.R.D. No. 12, No. T.D.

[4] *Entrop v. Imperial Oil, supra* note 1.

[5] *Imperial Oil Ltd. v. Communications, Energy, and Paperworkers Union of Canada, Local 614*, [1996] B.C.L.R.B.D. No. 257 (B.C. Labour Relations Board) at para. 5.; also see Cdn Civil Liberties Assn. v. Toronto Dominion Bank, supra note 3, and Entrop v. Imperial Oil, supra note 1.

[6] *Ontario (Human Rights Commission) v. Etobicoke (Borough)*, [1982] 1 S.C.R. 202.

[7] Cdn. *Civil Liberties Assn v. Toronto Dominion Bank, supra* note 3.

[8] *British Columbia (Public Service Employee Relations Commission) v. B.C.G.S.E.U.*, (1999) 176 D.L.R. (4th) 1 (S.C.C.).

[9] *Handfield v. Board of School Trustees, School District #26 (North Thompson)*, unreported, January 25, 1995 (B.C. Human Rights Council).

[10] *British Columbia (Superintendent of Motor Vehicles) v. British Columbia (Council of Human Rights)*, [1999] 3 S.C.R. 3.

[11] *Alberta Human Rights Commission v. Central Alberta Dairy Pool*, [1990] 2 S.C.R. 489.

[12] *Handfield v. Board of School Trustees, School District #26 (North Thompson), supra* note 9.

◆

ONTARIO HUMAN RIGHTS COMMISSION

DISABILITY AND THE DUTY TO ACCOMMODATE (2000)

Introduction

Under the Ontario *Human Rights Code,*[1] everyone has the right to be free from discrimination because of handicap or perceived handicap in the social areas of employment, services, goods, facilities, housing, contracts and membership in trade and vocational associations. This right means that persons with disabilities[2] have the right to equal treatment, which includes the right to accessible workplaces, public transit, health services, restaurants, shops and housing.

Almost one-third of complaints filed with the Ontario Human Rights Commission are on the ground of disability. Most are in the area of employment, with services constituting the second largest area. For this reason, this Policy focuses on the workplace, with specific guidance to support employers, unions and employees in the fulfilment of their duties and rights under the *Code.*[3]

Accommodation with dignity is part of a broader principle, namely, that our society should be structured and designed for inclusiveness. This principle, which is sometimes referred to as integration, emphasizes barrier-free design and equal participation of persons with varying levels of ability. Integration is also much more cost effective than building parallel service systems, although it is inevitable that there will be times when parallel services are the only option. Inclusive design and integration are also preferable to "modification of rules" or "barrier removal", terms that, although popular, assume that the status quo (usually designed by able-bodied persons), simply needs an adjustment to render it acceptable. In fact, inclusive design may involve an entirely different approach. It is based on positive steps needed to ensure equal participation for those who have experienced historical disadvantage and exclusion from society's benefits.[4] The right to equality can be breached by a failure to address needs related to disadvantage. As the Supreme Court of Canada has observed:

> [T]he principle that discrimination can accrue from a failure to take positive steps to ensure that disadvantaged groups benefit equally from services offered to the general public is widely accepted in the human rights field.[5]

This positive approach is more effective because it is accessible and inclusive from the start. Employers and others who set standards or requirements "owe an obligation to be aware of both the differences between individuals, and differences that characterize groups of individuals. They must build conceptions of equality into workplace [or other] standards".[6] A proactive approach to disability accommodation is therefore necessary.

Those responsible for accommodation[7] should be aware of the standards for accommodation. The following guiding principles should be kept in mind:

- The needs of persons with disabilities must be accommodated in the manner that most respects their dignity, to the point of undue hardship.
- There is no set formula for accommodation — each person has unique needs and it is important to consult with the person involved.
- Taking responsibility and showing willingness to explore solutions is a key part of treating people respectfully and with dignity.
- Voluntary compliance may avoid complaints under the Code, as well as save the time and expense needed to defend against them.

1. WHAT IS DISABILITY?

1.1 The Definition in the Human Rights Code

Section 10 (1) of the Code defines "handicap" as follows:

> "because of handicap" means for the reason that the person has or has had, or is believed to have or have had,
>
> (a) any degree of physical disability, infirmity, malformation or disfigurement that is caused by bodily injury, birth defect or illness, and without limiting the generality of the foregoing, including diabetes mellitus, epilepsy, any degree of paralysis, amputation, lack of

physical co-ordination, blindness or visual impediment, deafness or hearing impediment, muteness or speech impediment, or physical reliance on a guide dog or on a wheelchair or other remedial appliance or device,

(b) a condition of mental retardation or impairment,

(c) a learning disability, or a dysfunction in one or more of the processes involved in understanding or using symbols or spoken language,

(d) a mental disorder, or

(e) an injury or disability for which benefits were claimed or received under the insurance plan established under the Workplace Safety and Insurance Act, 1997.

"Disability" should be interpreted in broad terms. It includes both present and past conditions, as well as a subjective component, namely, one based on perception of disability. Although sections 10(a) to (e) set out various types of conditions, it is clear that they are merely illustrative and not exhaustive. Protection for persons with disabilities under this subsection explicitly includes mental illness,[8] developmental disabilities and learning disabilities. Even minor illnesses or infirmities can be "disabilities", if a person can show that she was treated unfairly because of the perception of a disability.[9] Conversely, a person with an ailment who cannot show she was treated unequally because of a perceived or actual disability will be unable to meet even the *prima facie* test for discrimination. It will always be critical to assess the context of the differential treatment in order to determine whether discrimination has taken place, and whether the ground of disability is engaged.

1.2 A Broader Approach to Understanding Disability: A Social Perspective

The Supreme Court of Canada has recently shed new light on the approach to be taken in understanding disability. In *Mercier*,[10] a case arising in Quebec, the Supreme Court made it clear that disability must be interpreted to include its subjective component, since discrimination may be based as much on perceptions, myths and stereotypes, as on the existence of actual functional limitations.

In *Mercier*, the complainants were denied employment or dismissed when it was discovered that they had medical conditions. However, their conditions did not result in any functional limitations. The employers argued that since the conditions did not give rise to any functional limitations, they could not be "disabilities" under Quebec's human rights law. The Supreme Court of Canada disagreed.

The Court chose not to create an exhaustive definition of disability. Instead, it opted for an equality-based framework that takes into account evolving biomedical, social and technological developments. This includes a socio-political dimension that emphasizes human dignity, respect and the right to equality. Thus, a disability may be the result of a physical limitation, an ailment, a perceived limitation or a combination of all these factors. The focus is on the effects of the distinction, preference or exclusion experienced by the person and not on proof of physical limitations or the presence of an ailment.

Another Supreme Court of Canada decision[11] has since confirmed that "social handicapping", i.e., society's response to a real or perceived disability, should be the focus of the discrimination analysis.

This approach is consistent with the Code, which includes past, present and perceived conditions. It affords a broad and liberal interpretation and promotes the objectives of the *Code*.

1.3 Non-Evident Disabilities

The nature or degree of certain disabilities might render them "non-evident" to others. Chronic fatigue syndrome and back pain, for example, are not apparent conditions. Other disabilities might remain hidden because they are episodic. Epilepsy is one example. Similarly, environmental sensitivities can flare up from one day to the next, resulting in significant impairment to a person's health and capacity to function, while at other times, this disability may be entirely non-evident. Other examples might include:

- persons whose disabilities do not actually result in any functional limitations but who experience discrimination because others believe their disability makes them less able;
- persons who have recovered from conditions but are treated unfairly because of their past condition, and
- persons whose disabilities are episodic or temporary in nature.

Other disabilities may become apparent based on the nature of the interaction, such as when there is a need for oral communication with an individual who is deaf, or there is a need for written communication with an individual who has a learning disability. A disability might become apparent over time through extended interaction. It might only become known when a disability accommodation is requested or, simply, the disability might remain "non-evident" because the individual chooses not to divulge it for personal reasons.

Regardless of whether a disability is evident or non-evident, a great deal of discrimination faced by persons with disabilities is underpinned by social constructs of "normality" which in turn tend to reinforce obstacles to integration rather than encourage ways to ensure full participation. Because these disabilities are not "seen", many of them are not well understood in society. This can lead to stereotypes, stigma and prejudice.

1.4 Mental Disability

Although mental disability is a form of non-evident disability, it raises particular issues that merit independent consideration. Over the years, many employers have expressed the need for specific guidance on the issue of mental disability. Section 10 of the Code expressly includes mental disabilities. Persons with mental disabilities face a high degree of stigmatization and significant barriers to employment opportunities.[12] Stigmatization can foster a climate that exacerbates stress, and may trigger or worsen the person's condition. It may also mean that someone who has a problem and needs help may not seek it, for fear of being labelled.

The Supreme Court of Canada has recognized the distinct disadvantage and negative stereotyping faced by persons with mental disabilities, and has held that discrimination against individuals with mental disabilities is unlawful. In *Gibbs v. Battlefords* [13] the Court struck down an insurance plan for employees with disabilities that limited benefits for mental disabilities to a lower level as compared to physical disabilities. It is therefore the Commission's position that such distinctions are *prima facie* discriminatory.

2. *PRIMA FACIE* DISCRIMINATION BECAUSE OF DISABILITY

Once a disability within the meaning of section 10 of the *Code* is established, the individual has the burden of showing a *prima facie* case of discrimination.

Discrimination under the Code can be direct (refusal to grant a job or provide access to services or housing, for example, because of a disability), indirect, constructive (adverse effect) or based on society's failure to accommodate actual differences.

In some cases, it will be clear that discrimination has occurred. In others, a preliminary assessment tool may be helpful. The Supreme Court of Canada has suggested three broad inquiries to determine if discrimination has taken place:[14]

(1) Differential Treatment

Was there substantively differential treatment, either because of a distinction, exclusion or preference, or because of a failure to take into account the complainant's already disadvantaged position within Canadian society?

(2) An Enumerated Ground

Was the differential treatment based on an enumerated ground?

(3) Discrimination in a Substantive Sense

Finally, does the differential treatment discriminate by imposing a burden upon, or withholding a benefit from, an individual?. The discrimination might be based on stereotypes of a presumed group or personal characteristics, or might perpetuate or promote the view that an individual is less capable or worthy of recognition or value as a human being or as a member of Canadian society who is equally deserving of concern, respect and consideration. Does the differential treatment amount to discrimination because it makes distinctions that are offensive to human dignity?

Given the clear historical disadvantage experienced by persons with disabilities, it is likely that most differential treatment because of disability will result in a finding of *prima facie* discrimination.[15] This would include not only unfair treatment because of disability, but also neutral factors or requirements that have an adverse impact on persons with disabilities. It would also include inappropriate responses, or a lack of response to the complainant's condition or stated need for accommodation.

2.1 Discrimination and Insurance

Discrimination may also take place where a term or condition of employment requires enrolment in a group insurance contract and an applicant does not qualify for the insurance plan because of disability. The term or condition of employment itself would be viewed as a violation of the *Code*.[16]

If an employee is excluded because of a disability from a benefit, pension or superannuation plan or fund or a contract of group insurance, an employer must compensate the employee an amount equivalent to the contribution that the employer would have otherwise made on behalf of an employee who does not have a disability.[17]

Compensation to employees takes on different forms, such as contributions to benefit premiums or accrual of vacation credits. Where employers, as a matter of course, pay a certain form of compensation to other employees who are absent from work, employees absent due to disability are also entitled to such compensation.[18]

3. THE DUTY TO ACCOMMODATE

3.1 General Principles

3.1.1 Respect for Dignity

The duty to accommodate persons with disabilities means accommodation must be provided in a manner that most respects the dignity of the person, if to do so does not create undue hardship.[19] Dignity includes consideration of how accommodation is provided and the individual's own participation in the process.

Human dignity encompasses individual self-respect and self-worth. It is concerned with physical and psychological integrity and empowerment. It is harmed when individuals are marginalized, stigmatized, ignored or devalued.[20] Privacy, confidentiality, comfort, autonomy, individuality and self-esteem are important factors as well as to whether an accommodation maximizes integration and promotes full participation in society.

Different ways of accommodating the needs of persons with disabilities should be considered along a continuum from those ways which are most respectful of privacy, autonomy, integration and other human values, to those which are least respectful of those values.

Perhaps the most common example of an accommodation that demonstrates little respect for the dignity of a person with a disability is a wheelchair entrance over a loading dock or through a service area or garbage room. Persons with disabilities should have the same opportunity as others to enter a building in a manner that is as convenient and pleasant for them as it is for others.

3.1.2 Individualized Accommodation

The essence of accommodating people with disabilities is individualization. As a result of the new three-step test proposed by the Supreme Court of Canada and re-affirmed by the Ontario Court of Appeal in *Entrop*,[21] each person with a disability must be considered, assessed and accommodated individually.

Example: A corporate policy provides for obligatory termination in the event that an employee in a safety-sensitive position tests positive after a breathalyzer test. This blanket policy does not provide for individualized assessment or the appropriateness of the outcome in the circumstances and, accordingly, does not accommodate employees on an individual basis.

There is no set formula for accommodating people with disabilities. Each person's needs are unique and must be considered afresh when an accommodation request is made. A solution may meet one person's requirements but not another's, although it is also the case that many accommodations will benefit large numbers of persons with disabilities.

3.1.3 Integration and Full Participation

International human rights standards point to the importance of full participation and enjoyment of life for persons with disabilities. The United Nations' *Declaration of the Rights of Disabled Persons* [22] provides in sections 3 and 8 that:

> 3. Disabled persons have the inherent right to respect for their human dignity. Disabled persons, whatever the origin, nature and seriousness of their handicaps and disabilities, have the same fundamental rights as their fellow citizens of the same age, which implies first and foremost the right to enjoy a decent life, as normal and full as possible.
>
> [...]
>
> 8. Disabled persons are entitled to have their special needs taken into consideration at all stages of economic and social planning.

With these principles in mind, achieving integration and full participation for persons with disabilities requires barrier-free and inclusive designs and removal of existing barriers. Preventing and removing barriers means persons with disabilities should be able to access their environment and face the same duties and requirements as everyone else with dignity and without impediment. Where barriers continue to exist because it is impossible to remove those barriers at a given point in time, then accommodation should be provided to the extent possible, short of undue hardship.

It is well established in human rights law that equality may sometimes require different treatment that does not offend the individual's dignity. In some circumstances, the best way to ensure the dignity of persons with disabilities may be to provide separate or specialized services. However, employment, housing, services and facilities must be built or adapted to accommodate individuals with disabilities in a way that promotes their integration and full participation. Segregated treatment in services, employment, or housing for individuals with disabilities is less dignified and is unacceptable, unless it can be shown that integrated treatment would pose undue hardship or that segregation is the only way to achieve equality.[23]

3.1.3(a) Design by Inclusion

Integration requires up front barrier-free design and inclusion-by-design in order to fully integrate persons with disabilities into all aspects of society as much as possible.

This approach combats "social handicapping" and recognizes that social attitudes and actions often contribute to "handicaps": a person may have few or even no limitations other than those created by non-inclusive thinking. The Supreme Court has noted the need to "fine-tune" society so that structures and assumptions do not exclude persons with disabilities from participation in society[24] and it has more recently affirmed that standards should be designed to reflect all members of society, insofar as this is reasonably possible.[25]

When constructing new buildings, undertaking renovations, purchasing new computer systems, launching new Web sites, setting up new policies and procedures, offering new services, or implementing new public transit routes, design choices should be made that do not create barriers for persons with disabilities.

Inclusive design is the approach that is most respectful of the dignity of persons with disabilities.

3.1.3(b) Removing Barriers

Persons with disabilities are currently excluded by many kinds of barriers, including physical, attitudinal and systemic ones. Significant changes are required as part of the duty to accommodate in order to provide equal access to employment (including collective agreements), transportation systems, buildings (except private residences), rental accommodation, services, restaurants, shopping centres, stores and other places and activities. These changes are necessary in order to give meaning to the right to equality and freedom from discrimination guaranteed to persons with disabilities under Part I of the *Code*.

A systemic barrier is not just a single rule or policy but a combination of policies and/or guidelines that result in the exclusion of people identified by a *Code* ground such as disability.

Organizations should understand and be aware of the possibility that systemic barriers may exist within their organization and actively seek to identify and remove them.

Barrier removal maximizes integration with one's environment so ideally everyone is able to participate fully and with dignity. Identifying and removing systemic barriers also makes good business sense. It may reduce and prevent the filing of human rights complaints and can make facilities and procedures more comfortable for other groups such as seniors and for all people in general.

3.1.3(c) Accommodating Remaining Needs

Even up-front barrier-free or inclusive design and systematic removal of existing barriers may not result in full participation for persons with disabilities. At this point, differential treatment might be required in order to provide equal opportunity to full participation.

Again, accommodating remaining needs through differential treatment must be done in a manner that maximizes integration and dignity.

3.2 Legal Principles

Once a *prima facie* case of discrimination is found to exist, the legal burden shifts to the person responsible for accommodation to show that the discrimination is justifiable. The following sections will deal with the basic legal test that persons responsible for accommodation must meet, and with the shared responsibilities of all parties to the accommodation process.

Section 11 of the *Code*, combined with section 9, operates to prohibit discrimination that results from requirements, qualifications, or factors that may appear neutral but which have an adverse effect on persons with disabilities. This is often called "adverse effect", or "constructive" discrimination. Section 11 allows the person responsible for accommodation to demonstrate that the requirement, qualification or factor is reasonable and *bona fide* by showing that the needs of the group to which the complainant belongs cannot be accommodated without undue hardship.

Section 17 also creates an obligation to accommodate, specifically under the ground of disability. Section 17 states that a right is not infringed if the person with a disability is incapable of performing or fulfilling the essential duties or requirements attending the exercise of the right. However, this defence is not available unless it can be shown that the needs of the person cannot be accommodated without undue hardship.

Section 17 addresses two important differences between disability and other *Code* grounds.[26] Firstly, it recognizes that discrimination against persons with disabilities is not always grounded in negative stereotypes but rather can be based on society's failure to accommodate actual differences. Secondly, it emphasizes the need for individualized accommodation, because the ground of disability "means vastly different things depending upon the individual and the context".[27]

The Ontario Court of Appeal has confirmed recently that both sections 11 and 17 apply to persons with disabilities.[28] However, as a result of two landmark decisions of the Supreme Court of Canada,[29] the distinction between direct discrimination and adverse effect discrimination has become of much less practical significance. The Ontario Court of Appeal has confirmed that this "unified approach" should be applied to Ontario human rights law as well.[30] The practical result is that in most cases of discrimination on the ground of disability, individualized accommodation will be necessary.

The Supreme Court of Canada sets out a framework for examining whether the duty to accommodate has been met.[31] If *prima facie* discrimination is found to exist, the person responsible for accommodation must establish on a balance of probabilities that the standard, factor, requirement or rule

1. was adopted for a purpose or goal that is rationally connected to the function being performed,

2. was adopted in good faith, in the belief that it is necessary for the fulfilment of the purpose or goal, and
3. is reasonably necessary to accomplish its purpose or goal, in the sense that it is impossible to accommodate the claimant without undue hardship.

As a result of this test, the rule or standard itself must be inclusive and must accommodate individual differences up to the point of undue hardship rather than maintaining discriminatory standards supplemented by accommodation for those who cannot meet them. This ensures that each person is assessed according to his or her own personal abilities instead of being judged against presumed group characteristics.[32]

The ultimate issue is whether the person responsible for accommodation has shown that accommodation has been provided up to the point of undue hardship. In this analysis, the procedure to assess accommodation is as important as the substantive content of the accommodation.[33]

The following non-exhaustive factors should be considered in the course of the analysis:[34]

- whether the person responsible for accommodation investigated alternative approaches that do not have a discriminatory effect;
- reasons why viable alternatives were not implemented;
- ability to have differing standards that reflect group or individual differences and capabilities;
- whether persons responsible for accommodation can meet their legitimate objectives in a less discriminatory manner;
- whether the standard is properly designed to ensure the desired qualification is met without placing undue burden on those to whom it applies; and
- whether other parties who are obliged to assist in the search for accommodation have fulfilled their roles.

3.3 Most Appropriate Accommodation

The duty to accommodate requires that the most appropriate accommodation be determined and then be undertaken, short of undue hardship. The most appropriate accommodation is one that most respects the dignity of the individual with a disability, meets individual needs, best promotes integration and full participation, and ensures confidentiality.

Accommodation is a process and is a matter of degree, rather than an all-or-nothing proposition, and can be seen as a continuum. At one end of this continuum would be full accommodation that most respects the person's dignity. Next is phased-in accommodation over time, followed by the most appropriate accommodation only being implemented once sufficient reserve funds have been set aside. Alternative accommodation (that which would be less than "ideal") might be next on the continuum when the most appropriate accommodation is not feasible. Alternative accommodation might also be accomplished at a later date if immediate implementation would result in undue hardship. Or, alternative accommodation might be implemented as an interim solution while the most appropriate accommodation is being phased in or implemented at a later date.

Whether an accommodation is "appropriate" is a determination completely distinct and separate from whether the accommodation would result in "undue hardship" (the test that has to be met under sections 11 and 17(2) of the *Code*).

Accommodation will be considered appropriate if it will result in equal opportunity to attain the same level of performance, or to enjoy the same level of benefits and privileges experienced by others or if it is proposed or adopted for the purpose of achieving equal opportunity, and meets the individual's disability-related needs. If the accommodation meets the individual's needs and does so in a way that most respects dignity, then a determination can be made as to whether or not this "most appropriate" accommodation would result in undue hardship.

An Ontario Board of Inquiry has ruled that short of undue hardship, the highest point in the continuum of accommodation must be achieved.[35] However, if there is a choice between two accommodations which are equally responsive to the person's needs in a dignified manner, then those responsible are entitled to select the one that is less expensive or that is less disruptive to the organization.

3.3.1 Essential Duties and The Current Job

The *Code* guarantees equal treatment to all persons capable of performing the essential duties or requirements of the job or service. No one can be judged incapable of performing those duties until efforts have been made to accommodate the individual up to the point of undue hardship. The first step is to separate the essential from the non-essential duties of the job. Where possible, non-essential tasks can be reassigned to another person. The person with the disability should then be assessed in terms of his or her ability to perform the essential duties and, on that basis, accommodation should be considered.

There is little guidance as to how to distinguish between essential duties and others. In one Ontario Board of Inquiry decision, the word "essential" was defined as follows:

> "Essential" means that which is "needed to make a thing what it is; very important; necessary" -Synonyms are "indispensable, requisite, vital." Thus, peripheral or incidental, non-core or non-essential aspects of a job are not pertinent to a determination under [s. 17(1)].[36]

Conclusions about inability to perform essential duties should not be reached without actually testing the ability of the person. It is not enough for the employer or person to assume that the person cannot perform an essential requirement. Rather, there must be an objective determination of that fact.[37]

The duty to accommodate may require employers to consider modifying performance standards or productivity targets. The term "performance standard" refers broadly to qualitative or quantitative standards that may be imposed on some or all aspects of work, whether they are set by the employer or through collective bargaining. A productivity target is a performance standard that relates specifically to the output of work expected by the employer. Performance standards generally can be distinguished from qualification standards, which are the skills or attributes that one must have to be eligible for a particular job:

> Production standards identify the level at which an employee must perform job functions in order to perform successfully. Qualification standards, on the other hand, identify the skills and abilities necessary to perform the functions at the required level.[38]

The central issue in determining whether or how performance standards should be modified is whether the standards in question are essential duties or requirements within the meaning of section 17 of the *Code*. If the person is unable to perform the standard, but the standard is not considered an essential part of the job, it can be changed or the function removed from the employee altogether and reassigned.

If the standard is essential, the employer is nevertheless required to accommodate the employee under section 17(2) of the *Code*. Keeping in mind the overall objective of the inclusion of employees with disabilities in the workplace, sections 17 (1) and (2) of the Code together include an obligation on an employer to accommodate a person. This accommodation may include an adjustment of that performance standard so long as doing so does not result in undue hardship. If it does amount to undue hardship, the employer has a defence.

This does not preclude the employer from enforcing performance standards that are unrelated to the disability. The employer is entitled to a productive employee and to develop standards and targets that maximize organizational objectives.

3.3.2 Alternative Work

Although accommodation in the pre-disability job is always preferable, it may not always be possible. The issue of whether an employee is entitled to have access to a job other than the pre-disability job is a matter of some debate. Nothing in the *Code* or in section 17 specifically restricts the requirement to accommodate a worker with disability to the pre-disability position. Conversely, nothing in section 17 expressly authorizes it either. Nevertheless, in light of the broad and purposive interpretation that should be afforded to human rights legislation, it is the Commission's view that accommodation in a job other than the pre-disability job may be appropriate in some circumstances. Section 17 may therefore include access to alternative work. Some of the following considerations may assist employers in determining whether such accommodation is available under section 17(2).

The following questions should be considered:

- Is alternative work possible and available, at present or in the near future?
- If it is not available, can a new position be created without causing undue hardship?
- Does it require additional training and does the training impose undue hardship?
- Do the tasks performed match the job description, or is there flexibility in the workplace with regard to an employee's responsibilities?
- Does the alternative work policy contravene a collective agreement?
- What are the terms of the collective agreement or individual contract of employment?
- What are the past practices of the workplace? How interchangeable are workers? Do employees frequently change positions either per-

manently or temporarily for reasons other than disability accommodation?[39]

Depending on how the previous questions are answered, accommodation may therefore include job restructuring, reassignment to open positions, retraining for alternative positions or job bundling if that would not constitute undue hardship for the employer. This will depend on the circumstances of the employment and the labour environment at a given workplace. In the final analysis, the employee must be able to perform a useful and productive job for the employer.[40]

Three of these options are discussed in the following sections.

3.3.2(a) Temporary Alternative Work

The term "alternative work" means different work or work that does not necessarily involve similar skills, responsibilities, and compensation. Temporary alternative work may be an appropriate accommodation either in a return to work context, or in a situation where a disability renders an employee temporarily unable to accomplish the pre-disability job.

Temporary alternative work can be an appropriate accommodation to assist an individual where the nature of the disability and its limitations are temporary or episodic.

3.3.2(b) Permanent Alternative Work

An employer-initiated alternative work arrangement must consider the circumstances of the individual's return to work. When an employee asks to be reinstated in a previous position, the employer may make the appropriate inquiries to assess whether the employee is fully able to carry out the essential functions of the job. Whenever possible, the returning employee should be given an opportunity to prove his or her ability to perform the pre-disability job.[41]

Where the employee can no longer perform his or her current job and if alternative work is appropriate based on the analysis described above, the Commission is of the view that the employer should consider permanent alternative work. This is consistent with a line of labour arbitration cases that have found that the duty to accommodate may include significant workplace reorganization[42] as well as with the obligation to provide suitable work in order to satisfy the duty to re-employ injured workers.[43]

Reassignment to a vacant position should be considered an appropriate accommodation only when accommodation in the current position would cause undue hardship. The vacant position must be vacant within a reasonable amount of time, but the employer is not required to "promote" the employee. Reassignment is not available to job applicants. If reassignment creates a conflict because of a collective agreement, accommodation needs should prevail over the collective agreement. When reassignment takes place, the person must be qualified for the reassigned position. The vacant position must be equivalent to the current one, although a less equivalent position would be acceptable if no equivalent one exists.

3.3.3 Return to Work

Accommodating a person who has been absent from work may involve any of the above forms of accommodation but also raises unique issues. People who return to work after an absence related to a ground in the *Code* are protected by the *Code*.[44] They generally have the right to return to their jobs, and this is frequently referred to as the "pre-disability job". Both employers and unions must co-operate in accommodating employees who are returning to work. Accommodation is a fundamental and integral part of the right to equal treatment in the return to work context.

The right to return to work for persons with disabilities only exists if the worker can fulfil the essential duties of the job after accommodation short of undue hardship.[45] If a person cannot fulfil the essential duties of the job, despite the employer's effort to accommodate short of undue hardship, there is no right to return to work. As noted in the preceding section, there may also be a right to alternative work.

Under the *Code*, there is no fixed rule as to how long an employee with a disability may be absent before the duty to accommodate has been met. This will depend on the ability of the employee to perform the essential duties of the job considering the unique circumstances of every absence and the nature of the employee's condition, as well as circumstances in the workplace. Also important is the predictability of absence, both in regards to when it will end and if it may recur and the frequency of the absence. The employee's prognosis and length of absence are also important considerations. It is more likely that the duty to accommodate will continue with a better prognosis, regardless of the length of absence.

The duty to accommodate does not necessarily guarantee a limitless right to return to work. On the other hand, a return to work program that relies on arbitrarily selected cut-offs or that requires an inflexible date of return may be challenged as a violation of the *Code*. Ultimately the test of undue hardship is the relevant standard for assessing return to work programs.

3.4 Duties and Responsibilities in the Accommodation Process

The accommodation process is a shared responsibility. Everyone involved should co-operatively engage in the process, share information, and avail themselves of potential accommodation solutions.

The person with a disability is required to:

- advise the accommodation provider of the disability (although the accommodation provider does not generally have the right to know what the disability is);
- make her or his needs known to the best of his or her ability, preferably in writing, in order that the person responsible for accommodation may make the requested accommodation;
- answer questions or provide information regarding relevant restrictions or limitations, including information from health care professionals, where appropriate, and as needed;
- participate in discussions regarding possible accommodation solutions;
- co-operate with any experts whose assistance is required to manage the accommodation process or when information is required that is unavailable to the person with a disability;
- meet agreed-upon performance and job standards once accommodation is provided;[46]
- work with the accommodation provider on an ongoing basis to manage the accommodation process; and
- discuss his or her disability only with persons who need to know. This may include the supervisor, a union representative or human rights staff.

The *employer* is required to:

- accept the employee's request for accommodation in good faith, unless there are legitimate reasons for acting otherwise;
- obtain expert opinion or advice where needed;
- take an active role in ensuring that alternative approaches and possible accommodation solutions are investigated,[47] and canvass various forms of possible accommodation and alternative solutions, as part of the duty to accommodate;[48]
- keep a record of the accommodation request and action taken;

- maintain confidentiality;
- limit requests for information to those reasonably related to the nature of the limitation or restriction so as to be able to respond to the accommodation request;
- grant accommodation requests in a timely manner, to the point of undue hardship, even when the request for accommodation does not use any specific formal language; and
- bear the cost of any required medical information or documentation. For example, doctors' notes and letters setting out accommodation needs, should be paid for by the employer.

Unions and professional associations are required to:
- Take an active role as partners in the accommodation process;[49]
- share joint responsibility with the employer to facilitate accommodation;[50] and
- support accommodation measures irrespective of collective agreements, unless to do so would create undue hardship.

The duty to accommodate a disability exists for needs that are known. Organizations and persons responsible for accommodation are not, as a rule, expected to accommodate disabilities of which they are unaware. However, some individuals may be unable to disclose or communicate their needs because of the nature of their disability. In such circumstances, employers should attempt to assist a person who is clearly unwell or perceived to have a disability, by offering assistance and accommodation. On the other hand, employers are not expected to diagnose illness or "second-guess" the health status of an employee.

Example: An employer is unaware of an employee's drug addiction but perceives that a disability might exist. The employer sees that the employee is having difficulty performing, and is showing signs of distress. If the employer imposes serious sanctions or terminates the employee for poor performance, without any progressive performance management and attempts to accommodate, these actions may be found to have violated the *Code*.[51]

Before terminating or sanctioning an employee for "unacceptable behaviour", an employer might first consider whether the actions of the employee are caused by a disability, especially where the employer is aware or perceives that the employee has a disability. Employers should always inform all employees that a disability-related assessment or accommodation can be provided as an option to address performance issues. Progressive performance management and discipline as well as employee assistance supports ensure that all employees have a range of opportunities to address performance issues on an individualized basis before sanctions or termination are considered. For example, severe change in an employee's behaviour could signal to an employer that the situation warrants further examination.

Mental illness should be addressed and accommodated in the workplace like any other disability. In some cases, an employer may be required to pay special attention to situations that could be linked to mental disability. Even if an employer has not been formally advised of a mental disability, the perception of such a disability will engage the protection of the *Code*. Prudent employers should try to offer assistance and support to employees before imposing severe sanctions. It should be borne in mind that some mental illnesses may render the employee incapable of identifying his or her needs.

Example: John has bipolar disorder, which he has chosen not to disclose to his employer because he is concerned about how he would be treated at work if it were known that he had a mental disability. He experiences a crisis at work, followed by a failure to appear at work for several days. The employer is concerned about John's absence and recognizes that termination for failure to report to work may be premature. The employer offers John an opportunity to explain the situation after treatment has been received and the situation has stabilized. Upon learning that a medical issue exists, the employer offers assistance and accommodation.

Once disability-related needs are known, the legal onus shifts to those with the duty to accommodate. For example, counselling or referral through Employee Assistance Programs (EAPs) could be the solution for an underlying disability that might be aggravated by workplace or personal stress.

There may be instances where there is a reasonable and bona fide basis to question the legitimacy of a person's request for accommodation or the adequacy of the information provided. In such cases, the accommodation provider may request confirmation or additional information from a qualified health care professional in order to obtain the needed information. No one can be forced to submit to an independent medical examination, but failure to respond to reasonable requests may delay the provision of accommodation until such information is provided.

3.4.1 Confidentiality

Persons with disabilities are not necessarily required to disclose private or confidential matters, and should disclose information to the accommodation provider only as it pertains to the need for accommodation and any restrictions or limitations.

Example: An employee with AIDS has provided documentation to demonstrate her need for a flexible schedule and rest periods to manage periods of fatigue, and time to attend appointments with health care professionals. However, it is not necessary for the employee to disclose that she has AIDS. The employer is entitled to know that the employee has a disability and that she needs certain accommodations in order to remain productive at work.

Maintaining confidentiality for individuals with mental illness may be especially important because of the strong social stigmas and stereotyping that still persist about such disabilities.

Documentation supporting the need for particular accommodation (flexible hours, a different supervisor, a particular technical aid, for example) should be provided only to those who need to be aware of the information. It may be preferable in some circumstances for information to be provided to the company's health department or human resources staff rather than directly to the supervisor, so as to further protect confidentiality. Medical documentation should be kept separate from the person's corporate file.

4. UNDUE HARDSHIP

The *Code* prescribes three considerations in assessing whether an accommodation would cause undue hardship. These are:

- cost,
- outside sources of funding, if any, and
- health and safety requirements, if any.

Accommodating someone with a disability is seldom as expensive or difficult as is sometimes imagined. Over two-thirds of job accommodations cost under $500; many cost nothing at all.[52]

The *Code* sets out only three considerations. This means that no other considerations, other than those that can be brought into those three standards, can be properly considered under Ontario law. There have been cases originating from other jurisdictions or from Ontario prior to the amendment of the *Code* that have included such other factors as employee morale, or conflict with a collective agreement. However, the Ontario legislature has seen fit to enact a higher standard by specifically limiting undue hardship to three particular components. The broad and purposive interpretation of the *Code* and human rights generally means that rights must be construed liberally and defences to those rights should be construed narrowly.[53] Moreover, the *Code* has primacy over legislation,[54] and also prevails over agreements such as collective agreements.[55]

Several factors are therefore excluded from considerations that are frequently raised by respondents. These are business inconvenience, employee morale, customer preference, and collective agreements or contracts.[56]

4.1 Excluded Factors

4.1.1 Business Inconvenience

"Business inconvenience" is not a defence to the duty to accommodate. If there are demonstrable costs attributable to decreased productivity, efficiency or effectiveness, they can be taken into account in assessing undue hardship under the cost standard, providing they are quantifiable and demonstrably related to the proposed accommodation.

4.1.2 Employee Morale

In some cases, accommodating an employee may generate negative reactions from co-workers who are either unaware of the reason for the accommodation or who believe that the employee is receiving an undue benefit. The reaction may range from resentment to hostility. However, the person responsible for providing accommodation should ensure that staff are supportive and are helping to foster an environment that is positive for all employees. It is not acceptable to allow discriminatory attitudes to fester into workplace hostilities that poison the environment for disabled workers.

Moreover, individuals with disabilities have a right to accommodation with dignity. It is an affront to an individual's dignity if issues of morale and misconception stemming from perceived unfairness are not prevented or dealt with. In such cases, those responsible will not have met their duty to provide accommodation with dignity.

4.1.3 Third-Party Preference

Human rights case law notes that third party preferences do not constitute a justification for discriminatory acts, and the same rule applies to customer preferences.[57]

4.14 Collective Agreements or Contracts

Collective agreements or other contractual arrangements cannot act as a bar to providing accommodation. The Courts have determined that collective agreements and contracts must give way to the requirements of human rights law. To allow otherwise would be to permit the parties to contract out of their *Code* rights under the auspices of a private agreement. Accordingly, subject to the undue hardship standard, the terms of a collective agreement or other contractual arrangement cannot justify discrimination that is prohibited by the *Code*.

A union may cause or contribute to discrimination by participating in formulating a work rule, e.g. a provision in the collective agreement, that has a discriminatory effect.[58] Unions and employers are jointly responsible for negotiating collective agreements that comply with human rights laws. They should build conceptions of equality into collective agreements.[59]

Example: When a union and employer are negotiating a collective agreement, the principle of seniority is maintained as a general principle. However, the union and employer can together address how employees with disabilities will be accommodated.

However, if an employer and a union cannot reach an agreement on how to resolve an accommodation issue, the employer must make the accommodation in spite of the collective agreement. If the union opposes the accommodation, or does not co-operate in the accommodation process, then the union may be named as a respondent in a complaint filed with the Commission.

Unions will have to meet the same requirements of demonstrating undue hardship having regard to costs, and health and safety. For example, if the disruption to a collective agreement can be shown to create direct financial costs, this can be taken into account under the cost standard. Issues surrounding terms of a collective agreement relating to health or safety are dealt with under the section dealing with Health and Safety.

In non-unionized environments, employers can make flexible employment arrangements to meet their duty to accommodate. The same sort of flexible employment arrangements should be considered in unionized environments, although they may fall outside the collective agreement where the duty to accommodate arises.

4.2 Onus of Proof and Objective Evidence

In order to claim the undue hardship defence, the person who is responsible for making the accommodation has the onus of proof.[60] It is not up to the person with a disability to prove that the accommodation can be accomplished without undue hardship.

The nature of the evidence required to prove undue hardship must be objective, real, direct, and, in the case of cost, quantifiable. The person responsible for accommodation must provide facts, figures, and scientific data or opinion to support a claim that the proposed accommodation in fact causes undue hardship. A mere statement, without supporting evidence, that the cost or risk is "too high" based on impressionistic views or stereotypes will not be sufficient.[61]

Example: A deaf patient requires a sign language interpreter in a hospital. The hospital administrator refuses to provide the accommodation, stating "if everyone wanted signers, it would bankrupt us." The hospital administrator does not provide financial information to justify this claim, nor does he provide demographic evidence to show the likely number of patients who may require signers. As a result, the hospital's defence will be unlikely to succeed.

Objective evidence includes, but is not limited to:

- financial statements and budgets,
- scientific data, information and data resulting from empirical studies,
- expert opinion,
- detailed information about the activity and the requested accommodation,
- information about the conditions surrounding the activity and their effects on the person or group with a disability.

4.3 Elements of the Undue Hardship Defence

4.3.1 Cost

The Supreme Court of Canada has said that, "one must be wary of putting too low a value on accommodating the disabled. It is all too easy to cite increased cost as a reason for refusing to accord the disabled equal treatment".[62] The cost standard is therefore a high one.

Costs will amount to undue hardship if they are:

- quantifiable;
- shown to be related to the accommodation; and
- so substantial that they would alter the essential nature of the enterprise, or so significant that they would substantially affect its viability.

This test will apply whether the accommodation will benefit one individual or a group.

The costs that remain after all costs, benefits, deductions and other factors have been considered will determine undue hardship.

All projected costs that can be quantified and shown to be related to the proposed accommodation will be taken into account. However, mere speculation, for example, about monetary losses that may follow the accommodation of the person with a disability will not generally be persuasive.

The financial costs of the accommodation may include

- capital costs, such as the installation of a ramp, the purchase of screen magnification or software,
- operating costs such as sign language interpreters, personal attendants or additional staff time,
- costs incurred as a result of restructuring that are necessitated by the accommodation, and
- any other quantifiable costs incurred directly as a result of the accommodation.

Concerns may arise about the potential increase in liability insurance premiums by the perceived health and safety risks of having persons with disabilities on particular job sites. Increased insurance premiums or sickness benefits would be included as operating costs where they are quantified, such as actual higher rates (not hypothetical), and are shown not to be contrary to the principles in the *Code* with respect to insurance coverage.[63] Where the increased liability is quantifiable and provable, and where efforts to obtain other forms of coverage have been unsuccessful, insurance costs can be included.

For the purposes of determining whether a financial cost[64] would alter the essential nature or substantially affect the viability of the organization, consideration will be given to:

- the ability of the person responsible for accommodation to recover the costs of accommodation in the normal course of business (see section 4.4.1),
- the availability of any grants, subsidies or loans from the federal, provincial or municipal government or from non-government sources which could offset the costs of accommodation,
- the ability of the person responsible for accommodation to distribute the costs of accommodation throughout the whole operation (see section 4.4.2),
- the ability of the person responsible for accommodation to amortize or depreciate capital costs associated with the accommodation according to generally accepted accounting principles, and
- the ability of the person responsible for accommodation to deduct from the costs of accommodation any savings that may be available as a result of the accommodation, including:
  - tax deductions and other government benefits (see section 4.4.4),
  - an improvement in productivity, efficiency or effectiveness (see section 4.4.5),
  - any increase in the resale value of property, where it is reasonably foreseeable that the property might be sold,
  - any increase in clientele, potential labour pool, or tenants, and
  - the availability of the Workplace Safety and Insurance Board's Second Injury and Enhancement Fund[65] (see section 4.4.6).

Larger organizations, including businesses and governments, may be in a better position to set an example or provide leadership in accommodating persons with disabilities. Accommodation costs will likely be more easily absorbed by larger organizations. Large employers, for example, are more likely to have the opportunities and the means to provide employment opportunities for greater numbers of persons with disabilities in a manner that accommodates their needs.

Heritage Buildings

The accessibility of heritage buildings raises controversial issues. A general exemption from accessibility requirements for heritage properties is not included in the Policy because it would result in broad exclusions as more and more buildings gain protection because of their heritage status. In a situation involving a heritage property, it is recognized that the cost of making the proposed accommodation may be increased by the necessity to preserve defining historic design features. However, aesthetic features, in and of themselves, that are not historic design features, are not to be included in the assessment.

The test of altering the essential nature or substantially affecting the viability of the enterprise allows the preservation of the defining features of a heritage property to be taken into account as a justifiable factor in assessing undue hardship.

4.3.2 Outside Sources of Funding

The availability of outside sources of funding may alleviate accommodation costs.[66] Organizations can make use of outside resources in order to meet their duty to accommodate and must first do so before claiming undue hardship.

There are three potential sources of funding to consider:

1. Funds that may be available to the individual only, provided through government programs and that are linked to the individual's disability.

   Resources, such as services or programs, might be available to accommodate the needs of persons with disabilities that could also aid them at work, in their apartment or while accessing a service.

   Persons with disabilities might be expected to first avail themselves of outside resources available to them when making accommodation requests to an employer or service provider. However, such resources should most appropriately meet the accommodation needs of the individual, including respect for dignity.

2. Funds that would assist employers and service providers defray the cost of accommodation.

   Other outside accommodation resources might be available to an individual with a disability when more than one organization has an overlapping or interconnected sphere of responsibility for the duty to accommodate.

   Example: A lawyer who is deaf, and who works for a large law firm, receives real-time captioning or sign language interpreter accommodation funded and provided by a court. While the lawyer is acting in court, the court takes responsibility for the duty to accommodate, relieving the lawyer's employer of its responsibility during this time period only.

3. Funding programs to improve accessibility for persons with disabilities — a corporate or organizational responsibility.

Governments have a positive duty to ensure that services generally available to the public are also available to persons with disabilities. Governments should not be allowed to evade their human rights responsibilities by delegating implementation of their policies and programs to private entities.[67] An organization that assumes responsibility for a government program must attend to the accommodation needs of its users.

4.3.3 Health and Safety

Health and safety requirements may be contained in a law or regulation, or result from rules, practices or procedures that have been established independently or in conjunction with other businesses or services engaged in similar kinds of activity.

Organizations have a responsibility to undertake health and safety precautions that would ensure that the health and safety risks in their facilities or services are no greater for persons with disabilities than for others. Where a health and safety requirement creates a barrier for a person with a disability, the accommodation provider should assess whether the requirement can be waived or modified. If waiving the health and safety requirement is likely to result in a violation of the *Occupational Health and Safety Act* (OHSA), the employer should generate alternative measures based on the equivalency clauses of the OHSA.[68] The employer is required to show an objective assessment of the risk as well as demonstrate how the alternative measure provides equal opportunity to the person with a disability. The employer might be able to claim undue hardship after these measures were undertaken and a significant risk still remains.

4.3.3(a) *Bona fide* and Reasonable Requirements

Health and safety risks will amount to undue hardship if the degree of risk that remains after the accommodation has been made outweighs the benefits of enhancing equality for persons with disabilities. The person responsible for accommodation will have to satisfy the three-step test set out in Section 3.2.

Health and safety standards that are genuinely adopted for the protection of workers, clients or the public will usually meet the second step of the test. On the other hand, a standard that is established to circumvent human rights legislation will not meet this test.

The third step requires the organization to demonstrate that the standard is reasonably necessary and that accommodation cannot be accomplished without incurring undue hardship.

Health or safety risks that result in undue hardship could be reduced to acceptable levels over time, for example, by adding safety features, or changing job descriptions to accommodate an employee with a disability. Development of a new technology to allow an employee with a disability to operate certain machinery more safely, for example, may take some time. In principle, therefore, a person responsible for accommodation could be required to phase in an accommodation that would lessen the health or safety risk over time, provided that the delay is reasonable and justified in relation to the development time attributed to the accommodation.

4.3.3(b) Assumption of Risk

A person with a disability may wish to assume a risk. The risk created by modifying or waiving a health and safety requirement is to be weighed against the right to equality of the person with a disability. Where the risk is so significant as to outweigh the benefits of equality, it will be considered to create undue hardship.

In determining whether an obligation to modify or waive a health or safety requirement, whether established by law or not, creates a significant risk to any person, consideration will be given to:

- the significance, probability and seriousness of the risk;
- the other types of risks that the person responsible for accommodation is assuming within the organization; and
- the types of risks tolerated within society as a whole, reflected in legislated standards such as licensing standards, or in similar types of organizations.

The "risk" that remains after all precautions including accommodations (short of undue hardship based on cost) have first been made to reduce the risk will determine undue hardship.

Where a modification or waiver of a health and safety requirement could place an individual with a disability at risk, the person responsible for accommodation is obliged to explain the potential risk to the individual. Where possible, persons with disabilities should be allowed to assume risk with dignity, subject to the undue hardship standard. At the same time, the organization has an obligation under health and safety legislation not to place individuals in a situation of direct threat of harm. High probability of substantial harm to any one will constitute an undue hardship.

Seriousness of the Risk

The fact that a person has a disability, in and of itself, is not sufficient to establish that there is a risk. Evidence will be required to prove the nature, severity, probability and scope of the risk.

In determining the seriousness or significance of a risk, the following factors should be considered:

- the nature of the risk
    - what could happen that would be harmful?
- the severity of the risk
    - how serious would the harm be if it occurred?
- the probability of the risk
    - how likely is it that the potential harm will actually occur?
    - is it a real risk, or merely hypothetical or speculative?
    - could it occur frequently?
- the scope of the risk
    - who will be affected by the event if it occurs?

These four factors should be considered together to determine the seriousness of the risk. If the potential harm is minor and not very likely to occur, the risk should not be considered to be serious. A risk to public safety shall be considered as part of the scope of the risk, while the likelihood that the harmful event may occur would be considered as part of the probability of risk. The seriousness of the risk is to be determined after accommodation and on the assumption that suitable precautions have been taken to reduce the risk.

Example: An ambulance dispatcher with a hearing impairment manages emergency calls over the telephone. Her capacity to do so safely and reliably is properly assessed while using a prescribed hearing aid and a hearing aid-compatible telephone.

Consideration of Other Types of Risk

When assessing the seriousness of the risk posed by the obligation to modify or waive a health or safety requirement, consideration must be given to the other types of risks that are assumed within an organization. For example, many jobs have risks that are inherent to the nature of the work itself.

As well, job applicants may be denied employment on the basis of limitations related to their disabilities. Yet these same or similar limitations may be developed by employees who have been on the job for several years, with little or no effect on their ability to satisfactorily perform their duties and with no impact on their careers.

Everyday Risk

Many sources of risk exist in the workplace, aside from those risks that may result from accommodating an employee with a disability. All employees assume everyday risks that may be inherent in a work site, or in working conditions, or which may be caused by a co-worker's fatigue, temporary inattentiveness, or stress. Employers have recognized that not all employees are 100% productive every day, and many provide counselling programs or other means of coping with personal problems, emotional difficulties or other problems that may arise. Risks created by these situations are factored into the level of safety or risk that we all accept in our lives every day.

A potential risk that is created by accommodation should be assessed in light of those other, more common sources of risk in the workplace.

Risks in Society as a Whole

Risks that are present in comparable enterprises or in society as a whole should be considered. While maximizing safety is always desirable, as a society we constantly balance the degree of safety to be achieved against competing benefits. For example, we balance the risk of injury in contact sports against the benefits of participating in sports activities or because of the economic and entertainment benefits. We balance the risks involved in permitting higher speed limits against the benefits of increasing the efficient flow of traffic. We balance the risks involved in driving affordable cars against the costs that would be involved in making them even safer.

4.4 Minimizing Undue Hardship

The following factors and strategies must be considered in order to avoid undue hardship and meet the duty to accommodate under the *Code*:

4.4.1 Cost Recovery

Persons responsible for accommodation should take steps to recover the costs of accommodation. For example, by making reasonable changes to business practices or obtaining grants or subsidies, the expense of making accommodation can be offset. If the person responsible for accommodation believes that such measures will not be effective in avoiding undue hardship, s/he will have to demonstrate that such steps to recover costs are inadequate in the circumstances, are impossible, or will not yield the needed resources.

In other words, the person responsible for accommodation would be required to establish that the costs, which remain after steps are taken to recover costs, will alter the essential nature or substantially affect the viability of the enterprise.

4.4.2 Distributing Costs

Costs of accommodation must be distributed as widely as possible within the organization responsible for accommodation so that no single department, employee, customer or subsidiary is burdened with the cost of an accommodation. The appropriate basis for evaluating the cost is based on the budget of the organization as a whole, not the branch or unit in which the person with disability works or to which the person has made an application. In the case of government, the term "whole operation" should refer to the programs and services offered or funded by the government. There may be accommodations that require substantial expenditure, which, if implemented immediately, would alter the essential nature of government programs or substantially affect their viability in whole or in part. In such instances, it may be necessary to implement the required accommodation incrementally.

4.4.3 Reducing Financial Burden

Organizations should consider spreading the financing of accommodation over time by taking out loans, issuing shares or bonds, or other business methods of financing. Amortization or depreciation is another means that an organization might be expected to use to reduce the financial burden, where possible.

4.4.4 Tax Deductions

Tax deductions or other government benefits flowing from the accommodation will also be taken into account as offsetting the cost of accommodation.

4.4.5 Improvements to Productivity, Efficiency, or Effectiveness

The person responsible for accommodation is expected to consider whether accommodation of the needs of a person with a disability may improve productivity, efficiency or effectiveness, expand the business, or improve the value of the business or property.

Example: An accommodation that affects a significant number of people with disabilities, such as persons requiring wheelchair access, could open up a new market for a storekeeper or a service provider. By building a ramp, several more persons will be able to access a store.

4.4.6 Second Injury and Enhancement Fund[69]

The effects of the Second Injury and Enhancement Fund of the Workplace Safety and Insurance Board (the "WSIB") must be considered. In the event of an injury to a worker, where the injury is caused by the worker's disability, a claim may be made against this fund even if the employer did not have knowledge of the employee's pre-existing condition. The rates for the employer will not be increased as a result of making claims on the fund.

Approximately 90% of employees in the province of Ontario are under the protection of the WSIB. Since the fund is available to most employers, there will be few instances where increased liability insurance premiums for risk of injury to a person due to a pre-existing condition or disability will be a factor in creating undue hardship.

4.4.7 Creative Design Solutions

Creative design solutions can often avoid expensive capital outlay. This may involve specifically tailoring design features to the individual's functional capabilities. Design solutions must be most respectful of dignity.

4.4.8 A Less Expensive Alternative

Where undue hardship is claimed, cost and risk estimates should be carefully examined to ensure that they are not excessive in relation to the stated objective. If so, a determination should be made as to whether a less expensive or lower risk alternative exists which could accomplish the accommodation (either as an interim measure to a phased-in solution or permanently) while still fully respecting the dignity of the person with a disability.

4.4.9 Phasing-in Accommodation

Some accommodations will be very important but will be difficult to accomplish in a short period of time.

Example: A small municipality may be able to show that to make its community centre or transportation system accessible in a single year would cause undue hardship. Or, a small employer may find it impossible to make its entrance and washroom facilities accessible immediately without undue hardship.

In these situations, undue hardship should be avoided by phasing in the accessible features gradually.

Some accommodations will benefit large numbers of persons with disabilities, yet the cost may prevent them from being accomplished. One approach, which may reduce the hardship, is to spread the cost over several years by phasing in the accommodation gradually.

Example: A commuter railroad might be required to make a certain number of stations accessible per year.

In many cases, while accommodation is being phased in over an extended period of time it may still be possible to provide interim accommodation for the individual. If both short and long-term accommodation can be accomplished without causing undue hardship, then both should be considered simultaneously.

4.4.10 Establishing a Reserve Fund

A second method of reducing the impact of the cost of an accommodation is to establish a reserve fund into which the person responsible for accommodation makes payment under specified conditions. One of the obvious conditions should be that the reserve fund is to be used only to pay for accommodation costs in the future. Accommodations could gradually be accomplished by expenditures out of the reserve fund or could eventually be accomplished once enough funds had been set aside.

A reserve fund should not be considered as an alternative to a loan where the accommodation could be made immediately and the cost paid back over time. Rather, the reserve fund is to be used in circumstances where it would create undue hardship for the person responsible for accommodation to obtain a loan and accomplish the accommodation immediately. The reserve fund is one of several financing options to be considered in assessing the feasibility of an accommodation. If a reserve fund is to be established, provision should be made for considering future changes in circumstances.

Both phasing in and the establishment of a reserve fund are to be considered only after the person responsible for accommodation has demonstrated that the most appropriate accommodation could not be accomplished immediately. Phasing in is to be preferred to the establishment of a reserve fund wherever possible.

4.4.11 Assessing the Impact of Remaining Costs

After all costs, benefits deductions, outside sources of funding, and other factors have been considered, the next step is to determine whether the remaining (net) cost will alter the essential nature or affect the viability of the organization responsible for making the accommodation.

The person responsible for accommodation would need to show how it would be altered or its viability affected. It will not be acceptable for the person responsible for accommodation to merely state, without evidence to support the statement, that the company operates on low margins and would go out of business if required to undertake the required accommodation.

Finally, if undue hardship can be shown, the person with a disability should be given the option of providing or paying for that portion of the accommodation that results in undue hardship.

4.4.12 Expert Assessment

Where an undue hardship analysis anticipates assessing substantial capital or operating expenditures or procedural changes, for example, in making physical alterations to an apartment building, work site, vehicle or equipment or changing health and safety requirements, it might be advisable for the person responsible for accommodation to obtain a proposal and estimate from experts in barrier-free design and construction.

5. ACCOMMODATION PLANNING AND IMPLEMENTATION

The best defence against human rights complaints is to be fully informed and aware of the responsibilities and protections included in the *Code*. Organizations can achieve this by developing disability accommodation policy and procedures as well as by conducting an accessibility review.

5.1 Organizational Policy

Organizations are responsible for dealing effectively, quickly and fairly with situations involving claims of harassment or discrimination. Organizations can be held liable by a court or tribunal if they or responsible staff members do not act to end discrimination or harassment in their workplaces.

When an act of harassment or discrimination or a need for accommodation is ignored, there are costs in terms of low morale, high stress, damaged professional reputations and employee absences.

Developing internal anti-discrimination policies and procedures to resolve complaints as part of a broad program to build a harassment-free and discrimination-free environment offers many benefits. Dealing promptly with these issues saves time and money. Letting people know the rules and defining unacceptable forms of behaviour makes it possible to avoid costly and upsetting hours in the courts or before specialized tribunals. In that way, strong policies and programs that prevent human rights complaints and help an organization effectively meet its duty to accommodate make good business sense.

The following should be part of any complete strategy to resolve human rights issues that arise in the workplace:

- anti-harassment or anti-discrimination policy;
- disability accommodation policy;
- a complaint resolution procedure; and
- ongoing education programs.

These elements should be developed in co-operation with the union or other workplace or organizational partners.

A disability accommodation policy should:

- outline rights and responsibilities
- require barrier analysis and prevention
- prepare and document accommodation plans
- monitor and evaluate implementation.

5.2 Accessibility Review

Organizations should consider developing accessibility review plans, undertaking reviews and implementing the necessary changes to make facilities, procedures and services accessible to employees, members, tenants, clients or customers with disabilities.

Conducting the accessibility review will show to what extent an organization is accessible to persons with disabilities and what needs to be done.

An accessibility review plan should:

- State the purpose of the review plan along with a rationale, context and guidance for conducting a review;
- Acknowledge an organization's obligations under the Code to ensure accessibility for employees, clients or customers with disabilities;
- Identify internal and external resources that would provide guidance for conducting the review;
- Summarize current internal and external initiatives;
- Identify quality service measures;
- Outline the scope of the review and identify potential barriers as they may relate to procedures and practices, facilities, services and communications;
- Outline timeframes and responsibilities around conducting an accessibility review of the organization;
- Outline a communications plan for the accessibility review so that senior management, staff, members, clients, etc. are aware and supportive of the initiative and its purpose.

Results of the accessibility review should be documented in a Summary of Findings and Recommendations Report and submitted to senior management. Senior management should make the results available to all concerned along with a plan for undertaking barrier-removal.

Accessibility review plans and barrier removal are up-front ways that an organization can address the needs of persons with disabilities. Developing and using a disability accommodation policy will also help an organization meet its duty to accommodate the individual needs of employees and customers with disabilities in accordance with the *Code*. Such a policy will make it clear to both employees with disabilities, others who require accommodation, and managers responsible for providing accommodation what company procedures are in place to assist persons with disabilities effectively.

ENDNOTES

[1]   R.S.O.1990, c. H.19.

[2]   The terms "disability" and "person with a disability" are used throughout this document instead of "handicap" or "handicapped person". Although the term "handicap" is used in the *Code*, many people with disabilities prefer the term "disability".

[3]   During consultations held in 1999 by the Ontario Human Rights Commission, stakeholders highlighted the particular issues facing educational institutions and those persons seeking access to them. Many of the principles set out in this Policy apply to service sectors as well, but the Commission will be undertaking new Guidelines for the educational sector in order to address these concerns.

[4]   In *Granovsky v. Canada (Minister of Employment and Immigration)*, 2000 SCC 28 (18 May 2000), online: Supreme Court of Canada <http://www.lexum.umontreal.ca/csc-scc/en/index.html> [hereinafter "*Granovsky*"], the Supreme Court recognized that the primary focus in the disability analysis is on the inappropriate legislative or administrative response (or lack thereof) of the State (at para. 39). The Court states (at para. 33):

> Section 15(1) ensures that governments may not, intentionally or **through a failure of appropriate accommodation**, stigmatize the underlying physical or mental impairment, or attribute functional limitations to the individual that the underlying physical or mental impairment does not entail, or fail to recognize the added burdens which persons with disabilities may encounter in achieving self-fulfillment in a world relentlessly oriented to the able-bodied.

> [emphasis added.]

Although in *Granovsky* the focus was State action, similar principles apply to persons responsible for accommodation under human rights law.

[5]   Eldridge v. British Columbia (Attorney General), [1997] 3 S.C.R. 624 at para. 78, online: <http://www.lexum.umontreal.ca/csc-scc/en/index.html> [hereinafter "*Eldridge*"].

6 *British Columbia (Public Service Employee Relations Commission) v. BCGSEU*, [1999] 3 S.C.R. 3 at para. 68 [hereinafter *"Meiorin"*].

7 The term "person (or organization or company) responsible for accommodation" includes individuals, partnerships, corporations, companies, unions, joint ventures and organizations. More than one "person" may be responsible for accommodation, and where this term is used, it refers to all parties who are obliged to take part in the accommodation.

8 Mental illness has been described as "significant clinical patterns of behaviour or emotions associated with some level of distress, suffering (pain, death), or impairment in one or more areas of functioning (school, work, social and family interactions). At the root of this impairment are symptoms of biological, psychological or behavioural dysfunction, or a combination of these." See Canadian Psychiatric Association, *Mental Illness and Work*, (brochure), online: Canadian Psychiatric Association homepage: http://cpa.medical.org/MIAW/MIAW.asp> at pg. 1

9 The *Code*'s definition of "handicap" includes perceived handicap.

10 *Quebec (Commission des droits de la personne et des droits de la jeunesse) v. Montréal (City)*; *Quebec (Commission des droits de la personne et des droits de la jeunesse) v. Boisbriand (City)*, 2000 SCC 27 (3 May 2000), online: Supreme Court of Canada http://www.lexum.umontreal.ca/csc-scc/en/index.html> [hereinafter *"Mercier"*].

11 *Granovsky, supra* note 4.

12 *Mental Illness and Work, supra* note 8.

13 *Gibbs v. Battlefords and Dist. Co-operative Ltd.* (1996), 27 C.H.R.R. D/87 (S.C.C.).

14 This was first articulated in *Law v. Canada (Minister of Employment and Immigration)*, [1999] 1 S.C.R. 497, online: Supreme Court of Canada <http://www.lexum.umontreal.ca/csc-scc/en/index.html> (date accessed: 4 August 2000) [hereinafter "Law"]. The approach has been affirmed in several subsequent cases, most notably two cases dealing with discrimination on the basis of disability: *Mercier, supra* note 10 and *Granovsky, supra* note 4.

15 The facts of *Granovsky, supra* note 4 illustrate an exception to this general proposition. Where a scheme targets a particular group, for example, those who are less fortunate than the complainant, it is unlikely to be considered discriminatory to exclude more advantaged groups.

[16] Subsection 25(1) of the *Code*.

[17] Subsection 25(4) of the *Code*.

[18] Conversely, in *O.N.A. v. Orillia Soldiers Memorial Hospital* (1999), 169 D.L.R. (4th) 489, leave to appeal to S.C.C. refused [1999] S.C.C.A. No. 118, online: QL (SCCA) [hereinafter "*Orillia*"], nurses on unpaid leave of absence due to disability did not accumulate service after periods set out in the collective agreement, and the employer was not required to contribute premiums to employee benefit plans after the employees had received long-term disability payments for a specified time. The Ontario Court of Appeal held that there was no contravention of the Code because these nurses were not treated differently from those in the appropriate comparator group, namely employees who were not working for other reasons.

[19] The Supreme Court's recent decisions in *Law, supra* note 14 and *Granovsky, supra* note 4 have confirmed that the concept of human dignity is central to discrimination analysis. These cases indicate that if an accommodation marginalizes, stigmatizes or demeans the person with a disability's sense of worth or dignity as a human being, it will not be appropriate. In commenting on the *Eaton* case, the Court said in *Granovsky, supra* note 4 at para. 74:

> ...Emily's claim might have succeeded if ...the Court had been persuaded that the Board's response to the challenge posed by Emily's placement [the accommodation] **had itself violated Emily's dignity as a human being equally deserving of consideration,** or placed discriminatory obstacles in the way of her self-fulfillment. [Emphasis added.]

[20] *Law, supra* note 14 at para. 53.

[21] *Entrop v. Imperial Oil Limited* (21 July 2000), Docket C29762 at para. 77-81 (Ont. C.A.), online: Court of Appeal for Ontario <http://www.ontariocourts.on.ca [hereinafter "*Entrop*"].

[22] United Nations, *Declaration of the Rights of Disabled Persons*, proclaimed by General Assembly resolution 3447 (XXX) of 9 December 1975.

[23] *Eaton v. Brant County Board of Education*, [1997] 1 S.C.R. 241 [hereinafter "*Eaton*"]. The Supreme Court stated that "integration should be recognized as the norm of general application because of the benefits it generally provides" (at para. 69), however, the Court found that in Emily Eaton's circumstances, segregated accommodation was in her best interests. The Court was of the view that this was one of those unusual cases where segregation was a more appropriate accommodation.

[24] *Eaton, ibid* at para. 67.

[25] *Meiorin, supra* note 6 at para. 68.

[26] *Eaton, supra* note 23 at para. 66-7. The unique nature of disability has been recognized by the Supreme Court of Canada.

[27] *Ibid*, at para. 69.

[28] *Supra, note* 21.

[29] *Meiorin, supra* note 6, and *British Columbia (Superintendent of Motor Vehicles) v. British Columbia (Council of Human Rights)*, [1999] 3 S.C.R. 868 [hereinafter *"Grismer"*].

[30] *Entrop v. Imperial Oil Limited* (21 July 2000), Docket C29762 at para. 77-81 (Ont. C.A.), online: Court of Appeal for Ontario <http://www.ontariocourts.on.ca [hereinafter *"Entrop"*].

[31] *Meiorin, supra* note 6.

[32] *Grismer, supra* note 29 at para. 20.

[33] *Ibid*, at para. 66.

[34] *Meiorin, supra* note 6 at para. 65.

[35] *Quesnel v. London Educational Health Centre*, (1995) 28 C.H.R.R. D/474 at para. 16 (Ont. Bd. of Inq.) [hereinafter *"Quesnel"*].

[36] *Cameron v. Nel-gor Nursing Home* (1984), 5 C.H.R.R. D/2170 at D/2192 (Ont. Bd. of Inq.) [dictionary citations omitted].

[37] *Ibid.* See also *Crabtree v. 671632 Ontario Ltd. (c.o.b. Econoprint (Stoney Creek)*, [1996] O.H.R.B.I.D. No. 37 (Ont. Bd. of Inq.), online: QL (HRBD).

[38] Robert L. Burgdorf, *Disability Discrimination in Employment Law* (Washington D.C.: Bureau of National Affairs, 1995) at 241.

[39] See M. K. Joachim, "The Duty to Accommodate Disabled Workers and the Provision of Alternative Work: An Unexplained Assumption" (2000) 7 Charter and Human Rights Litigation 407 for an excellent review of labour and human rights case law. Although Joachim locates the right to alternative employment in section 17(1), it can also be viewed as being located in the section 17(2) and the duty to accommodate. Whichever is the correct reasoning, employees should have some access to alternative employment.

[40] *Hamilton Civic Hospitals and CUPE, Local 794* (1994), 44 L.A.C. (4th) 31 [Ont. Arb. Award.]

[41] In *Chamberlin v. 599273 Ontario Ltd cob Stirling Honda* (1989), 11 C.H.R.R. D/110 (Ont. Bd. of Inq.), the Board of Inquiry found that the employer should have given the complainant the opportunity to prove he could still perform his old job.

[42] An employer may have to move an employee to a job more consistent with the employee's health status; *Re Calgary District Hospital Group and U.N.A. Loc. 121-R* (1994), 41 L.A.C. (4th) 319 (Alta. Lab. Rel. Bd.). The employer may have to look for work comparable to the original job rather than giving the employee an inferior position; *Re York County Hospital and Ontario Nurses' Association* (1992), 26 L.A.C. (4th) 384 (Ont. Lab. Rel. Bd.). The employer may even need to create a new job by joining together all the light duties and then reassigning the heavy duties to other employees; *Re Greater Niagara Hospital and Ontario Nurses Association* (1995), 50 L.A.C. (4th) 34 (Ont. Lab. Rel. Bd.). In one decision, the employer's duty to accommodate included not only the duties and requirements associated with the current job but also the duties and requirements associated with a bundle of tasks within the ability of an employee with a disability; *Re Mount Sinai Hospital and the O.N.A.* (1996), 54 L.A.C. (4th) 261 (Ont. Lab. Rel. Bd.).

[43] *Workplace Safety and Insurance Act*, S.O. 1997 c. 16 Sch. A, s. 40 and 41 [hereinafter "WSIA"].

[44] There are also rights and obligations pertaining to return to work set out in the WSIA that may exist concurrently with human rights protections.

[45] See Section 17 of the *Code*.

[46] In some cases, accommodation may require the modification of job standards. See the section entitled Essential Duties and the Current Job.

[47] *Meiorin, supra* note 6 at para. 65-66.

[48] Human Rights Digest, vol. 1 no. 2 (February/March 2000) citing *Conte v. Rogers Cablesystems Ltd.* (1999), C.H.R.R. Doc. 99-227 (Can. Human Rights Tribunal), *Mazuelos v. Clark* (2000) C.H.R.R. Doc. 00-011 (B.C. Human Rights Tribunal) and *Gordy v. Oak Bay Marine Management Ltd.* (2000) C.H.R.R. Doc. 00-040 (B.C. Human Rights Tribunal).

[49] The Supreme Court of Canada's decision in *Central Okanagan School District No. 23 v. Renaud*, [1992] 2 S.C.R. 970 [hereinafter "*Renaud*"] sets out the obligations of unions.

[50] *Ibid* at 988.

[51] For further information about drug and alcohol related disabilities, see Ontario Human Rights Commission, Policy on Drug and Alcohol

Testing (1996, revised September 27, 2000), Online: Ontario Human Rights Commission Web Site <http://www.ohrc.on.ca>.

[52] A. Cantor, "The Costs and Benefits of Accommodating Employees with Disabilities" (Toronto: 1996), online: Cantor + Associates Workplace Accommodation Consultants <http://www.interlog.com/~acantor/>.

[53] There are a number of cases that confirm this approach to the interpretation of human rights statutes. Most recently, in *Mercier, supra* note 10 the Supreme Court summarized these cases and outlined the relevant principles of human rights interpretation.

[54] Section 44 of the *Code*.

[55] *Renaud, supra* note 49.

[56] This is not an exclusive list. During the consultations, the issue of whether academic freedom may be a component of undue hardship was raised. Academic freedom is unrelated to the duty to accommodate and should not be a defence to accommodating persons with disabilities. For example, a student may require a more accessible classroom, or need more time in an examination because of a disability-related need. These are legitimate requests that do not diminish academic freedom. If an accommodation need places such a financial burden on the institution that it would amount to undue hardship by reason of cost or because it would substantially change the nature of the enterprise, or its viability, it would then meet the undue hardship standard. This issue will be dealt with at greater length in the Commission's planned guidelines on accommodation in the educational sector.

[57] The issue of customer, third party and employee preference is discussed in J. Keene, *Human Rights in Ontario*, 2nd ed. (Toronto: Carswell, 1992) at 204-5.

[58] *Renaud, supra* note 49.

[59] *Meirion, supra* note 6 at para. 68. Those setting standards and rules must be aware of the differences between individuals and groups of individuals. Standards and rules should not just be based on the 'mainstream' e.g. employees who do not have disabilities.

[00] *Grismer, supra* note 29 at para. 42.

[61] *Meiorin, supra* note 6 at para. 78-79 and *Grismer, supra* note 29 at para. 41. Cases since *Meiorin* and *Grismer* have also applied this stringent requirement for objective evidence; see, for example, *Miele v. Famous Players Inc.* (2000), 37 C.H.R.R. D/1 (B.C.H.R.T.).

[62] *Grismer, supra* note 32 at para. 41

[63] Section 25(1) of the *Code*.

[64] For further discussion on minimizing costs, please refer to section 4.4 "Minimizing Undue Hardship".

[65] Second Injury and Enhancement Fund (S.I.E.F), Policy Document (08-01-05) in the Pre-Bill 99 Operational Policy Manual of the Workplace Safety and Insurance Board (W.S.I.B).

[66] The Access Fund is an example of an outside source of funding. It helps community organizations develop barrier-free facilities, so persons with disabilities can be active volunteers and participate in potential employment opportunities. The Access Fund is part of Ontario's Equal Opportunity and Disability Partnerships and designed in partnership with the Ontario Trillium Foundation, which delivers the program.

[67] See *Eldridge, supra* note 5.

[68] R.S.O. 1990 c. 0-1. The OHSA regulations have equivalency clauses that allow for the use of alternative measures to those specified in its regulations, provided the alternative measures afford equal or better protection to workers.

[69] *Supra*, note 65.

♦

ONTARIO HUMAN RIGHTS COMMISSION

DRUG AND ALCOHOL TESTING (2000)

Introduction

The Commission recognizes that it is a legitimate goal for employers to have a safe workplace. One method sometimes used by employers to achieve that goal is drug and alcohol testing. However, such testing is controversial and, especially in the area of drug testing, of limited effectiveness as an indicator of impairment. It is not used to a significant degree anywhere in the world except in the United States (the "U.S.").[1]

It is the Commission's view that such testing is *prima facie* discriminatory and can only be used in limited circumstances. The primary reason for conducting such testing should be to measure impairment.[2] Even testing that measures impairment can be justified only if it is demonstrably connected to the performance of the job, for example, if an employee occupies a safety-sensitive position, or after significant accidents or "near-misses", or if there is reasonable cause to believe that a person is abusing alcohol or drugs and only then as part of a larger assessment of drug and alcohol abuse. It is the Commission's view that by focusing on testing that actually measures impairment, especially in jobs that are safety sensitive, an appropriate balance can be struck between human rights and safety requirements, both for employees and for the public.

Scope of this Policy

Persons with disabilities, who have had disabilities, or who are perceived to have or have had disabilities are protected against discrimination in all of the social areas of the *Code*.

Drug and alcohol testing are of particular concern in the workplace, notably for those Ontario employers who have safety sensitive operations, and/or that are subject to U.S. regulatory requirements (e.g. the trucking industry)[3] or to the policies of U.S. affiliates with "zero tolerance" for the consumption of drugs or alcohol. For this reason, this policy focuses on the workplace. However, it applies to other social areas as well.[4] For example, the Commission has taken the position that drug or alcohol testing as a prerequisite to eligibility for basic income support programs is also *prima facie* discriminatory.[5]

It should be noted that international and interprovincial transportation companies are under federal jurisdiction.[6] Thus airlines, interprovincial trucking and bus services are subject to the federal *Canadian Human Rights Act*[7] and not provincial human rights laws.

Drug or Alcohol Dependency and Abuse as a Disability[8]

Section 5(1) of the *Code* prohibits discrimination in employment on several grounds including "handicap" (the *Code* uses the term "handicap" but the more currently accepted term is "disability" and it is therefore used in this and other Commission documents). The *Code* adopts an expansive definition of the term "handicap" which encompasses physical, psychological and mental conditions. Severe substance abuse is classified as a form of substance dependence,[9] which has been recognized as a form of disability. Examples include alcoholism and the abuse of legal drugs (e.g. over the counter drugs) or illicit drugs. These types of abuse and dependence therefore constitute a disability within the meaning of the *Code*.

The following examples represent situations in which the use of legal or illicit drugs or alcohol may fall within the *Code*:[10]

(a) Where an individual's use of drugs or alcohol has reached the stage that it constitutes severe substance abuse, addiction or dependency, e.g. maladaptive patterns of substance use leading to significant impairment or distress, including:

    i) recurrent substance abuse resulting in a failure to fulfil major obligations at work;

    ii) recurrent substance abuse in situations which are physically hazardous;

    iii) continued substance abuse despite persistent social, legal or interpersonal problems caused or aggravated by the effects of the substance.[11]

(b) Where an individual is perceived as having an addiction or dependency due to drug or alcohol use, the *Code* will protect that individual.

Example: An employer refuses to promote a particular employee because of the perception that the employee has an alcohol dependency. As a result of this perception and consequent action on the part of the employer, the individual's right to equal treatment under the *Code* may have been infringed.

(c) An individual who has had a drug or alcohol dependency in the past, but who no longer suffers from an ongoing disability, is still protected by the *Code*.

Drug and Alcohol Testing: Direct or Constructive Discrimination?

Although the *Code* distinguishes between direct and constructive discrimination,[12] the distinction is less important than it used to be, particularly in the area of disability. This is a result of the combined impact of two factors. First, the Supreme Court of Canada has blurred the distinction between the two for practical purposes and has developed a single three-step test.[13] The Ontario Court of Appeal has applied similar reasoning in the Ontario context, specifically in the area of disability and drug and alcohol testing.[14]

Second, Section 17 of the *Code* provides a defence where a person with a disability is unable to perform an essential requirement. However, the defence is only available if the requirement is *bona fide* and reasonable, and only after the person has been accommodated to the point of undue hardship. Since employers usually argue that the requirement for impairment-free performance is essential, s. 17 of the *Code* will be an important part of a respondent's defence.

In either event, the Ontario Court of Appeal has indicated that except in the most obvious cases of direct discrimination, the focus should be on determining whether the employer can justify the policy or standard using the new three-step test set out by the Supreme Court of Canada.[15] Applying this approach, company-wide policies such as drug and alcohol testing policies will attract the need to accommodate employees and, most importantly, on an individual basis.[16] The Commission supports this position. Individualisation is central to the notion of dignity for persons with disabilities and to the concept of accommodation on the ground of disability, regardless of whether a particular form of drug testing or alcohol testing is likely to be considered to be "direct" or "constructive".[17] "Blanket" rules that make no allowances for individual circumstances are necessarily unable to meet individual requirements and are therefore likely to be struck down.

Drug and Alcohol Testing: Basic Principles

Drug and alcohol testing is *prima facie* discriminatory under Canadian human rights law. Employers can nevertheless justify discriminatory rules if they can meet a three-part test:[18]

- the employer has adopted the standard or test for a purpose that is rationally connected to the performance of the job;
- the employer adopted the particular standard or test in an honest and good faith belief that it was necessary to the fulfilment of that legitimate work-related purpose; and
- the standard or test is reasonably necessary to the accomplishment of that legitimate work-related purpose. To show that the standard is reasonably necessary, it must be demonstrated that it is impossible to accommodate individual employees sharing the characteristics of the claimant without imposing undue hardship upon the employer.

Drug and alcohol testing policies are part of workplace rules and standards. Therefore, standards governing the performance of work should be inclusive. Employers must build conceptions of equality into workplace policies.

Drug and alcohol testing should be limited to determining actual impairment of an employee's ability to perform or fulfil the essential duties or requirements of the job. It should not be directed towards simply identifying the presence of drugs or alcohol in the body.

Drug and alcohol testing that has no demonstrable relationship to job safety and performance has been found to be a violation of employee rights(19). A relationship or rational connection between drug or alcohol testing and job performance is an important component of any lawful drug or alcohol testing policy. In this regard, the policy must not be arbitrary in terms of which groups of employees are subject to testing. For example, to test only new or returning employees but not other employees may not be justifiable having regard to the stated objectives of a company's testing policy. At the same time, testing employees in safety sensitive positions only may be justifiable.

Applying the three-part test to drug and alcohol testing, the following questions should be considered by employers, where applicable:

i) Is there an objective basis for believing that job performance would be impaired by drug or alcohol dependency? In other words, is there a rational connection between testing and job performance?

ii) In respect of a specific employee, is there an objective basis for believing that unscheduled or recurring absences from work, or habitual lateness to work, or inappropriate or erratic behaviour at work are related to alcoholism or drug addiction/dependency? These factors could demonstrate a basis for "for cause" or "post incident" testing provided there is a reasonable basis for the conclusions drawn.

iii) Is there an objective basis to believe that the degree, nature, scope and probability of risk caused by alcohol or drug abuse or dependency will adversely affect the safety of co-workers or members of the public?

Pre-Employment Testing for Drug and Alcohol Use as Part of an Employment-Related Medical Examination

Testing for alcohol or drug use is a form of medical examination. Therefore, an employer considering such testing should be guided by the three-part test cited above, by the Commission's Policy on Employment-Related Medical Information[20] and by the Ontario Court of Appeal's recent decision in the *Entrop* case. The following are the main principles that should be borne in mind:

i) Employment-related medical examinations or inquiries, conducted as part of the applicant screening process, are prohibited under Section 23(2) of the *Code*

ii) Pre-employment medical examinations or inquiries at the interview stage should be limited to determining an individual's ability to perform the essential duties of a job.

iii) In order to implement a testing program prior to hiring, the employer must therefore be able to demonstrate that pre-employment testing provides an effective assessment of the applicant. Since drug testing cannot be shown to actually measure impairment, pre-employment drug testing should not be conducted. Although there has been no clear indication from the courts, it is the Commission's view that, in the absence of clear medical research, pre-employment alcohol testing does not appear to predict an employee's ability to perform the essential requirements of a safety-sensitive position. All it can do is assess impairment before the person is actually on the job. It is therefore difficult to see how an employer could justify pre-employment alcohol testing.

iv) Medical examinations to determine an individual's ability to perform the essential duties of a job should only be administered after a conditional offer of employment has been made, preferably in writing.

v) Where drug or alcohol testing will be a valid requirement on the job, the employer should notify job applicants of the requirement at the time that an offer of employment is made. The circumstances under which such testing might be required should be made clear to the applicant.

vi) If the applicant or employee requests accommodation in order to enable him or her to perform the essential duties of the job, the employer is required to provide individual accommodation unless it is impossible to do so without causing undue hardship.

On-the-Job Testing

On-the-job testing should be administered only where a link has been established between impairment and performance of job functions, such as in the case of employees who are in safety sensitive positions. Once again, because drug tests do not actually measure impairment, random drug testing is an unjustifiable intrusion into the rights of employees. With respect to random alcohol testing, the use of breathalysers is a minimally intrusive yet highly accurate measure of both consumption and actual impairment. Consequently, the Commission supports the view that random alcohol testing is acceptable in safety sensitive positions, especially where the supervision of staff is minimal or non-existent, but only if the employer meets its duty to accommodate the needs of those who test positive (see below).

"For cause" and "post incident" testing for either alcohol or drugs may be acceptable in specific circumstances. Following accidents or reports of dangerous behaviour, for example, an employer will have a legitimate interest in assessing whether the employee in question had consumed substances that are psychoactive and which may have contributed to the incident. The results of the assessment may provide an explanation of the cause of the accident. Such testing should only be conducted as part of a larger assessment of drug or alcohol abuse. This larger assessment could

154

include a broader medical assessment under a physician's care where there are reasonable grounds to believe that there is an underlying problem of substance abuse. Additional components of a larger assessment may include employee assistance programs ("EAPs"), peer reviews and supervisory reviews.

Employers should also have regard to the following criteria and considerations when developing on-the-job testing criteria:

1. Competent Handling of Test Samples

Qualified professionals must perform drug and alcohol testing and the results must be analysed in a competent laboratory. Further, it is the responsibility of the employer to ensure that the samples taken are properly labelled and protected at all times.

2. Confidentiality of Test Results

In order to protect the confidentiality of test results, all health assessment information should remain exclusively with the examining physician and away from the employee's personnel file.

3. Review of Results with the Employee

Procedures should be instituted for the physician to review the test results with the employee concerned.

4. Mandatory Self-Disclosure

Where mandatory self-disclosure is a part of a workplace drug or alcohol policy, there must be a reasonable time period within which previous substance abuse will be considered relevant to assessment of current ability to perform the essential duties. The reasonable time period is based on whether the risk of relapse or recurrence is greater than the risk that a member of the general population will suffer a substance abuse problem. Mandatory self-disclosure of all previous substance dependencies, without any reasonable limitation on how long ago these conditions occurred, has been found to be a *prima facie* violation of employee rights.[21]

5. Alternative Methods

The Commission supports the use of methods other than drug and alcohol testing (e.g. functional performance testing) where such methods exist, or the development of such tests, where feasible, to assess impairment. The Commission also encourages the development and implementation of EAPs and peer monitoring.

Consequences of a Positive Test

Section 17 of the *Code* requires individualized or personalized accommodation measures. Therefore, policies that result in automatic loss of employment, reassignment or that impose inflexible reinstatement conditions, without regard for personal and individual circumstances, are unlikely to meet this requirement.[22]

Although the emphasis in the *Code* is on ensuring that persons with disabilities are not treated in a discriminatory manner because of their disability, it is recognized that in some circumstances, the nature and/or degree of a person's disability may preclude that individual from performing the essential duties of a job. Section 17(1) of the *Code* states that the right to equal treatment in respect of employment is not infringed where an individual is treated differently because she or he is incapable of performing or fulfilling the essential duties of the position because of a disability. Assessment of incapacity must be both fair and accurate.

Duty to Accommodate

1. Section 17(2)

Section 17(2) provides that an employee shall not be found incapable of performing the essential duties of a job unless it would cause undue hardship to accommodate the individual employee's needs, taking into account the cost of the accommodation and health and safety concerns.

Sections 17(1) and 17(2) provide a two-stage test for the validity of a workplace drug and alcohol testing policy.

Example: An employer is concerned about fairness and decides to extend an existing alcohol testing policy originally designed for employees in safety-sensitive positions to cover all other employees. Although the policy's generous rehabilitation programs may satisfy the accommodation

156

requirement set out in Section 17(2), this defence is not available to the employer unless it can be shown that employees in non-safety-sensitive positions who fail the test are incapable of performing their essential duties.

2. Onus on the Employee to Co-operate with the Employer

A person who requires accommodation in order to perform the essential duties of a job has a responsibility to communicate the need for accommodation in sufficient detail and to co-operate in consultations to enable the person responsible for accommodation to respond to the request. It should be noted that this obligation does not interfere with the employer's obligation to treat the person equally even if the employer believes or perceives (even with good reason) that the employee has substance abuse problem.

Example: An employee in a clerical position appears to be inebriated frequently during work hours, and the employer has a conversation to address the problem. The employee refuses to acknowledge the problem or seek counselling at the employer's expense. Shortly after, the employee is fired without formal warning.

In this case, the employer clearly "perceived" the person to have a substance abuse problem and therefore the protection of the *Code* is engaged. The fact that a person refuses treatment or accommodation does not in and of itself justify immediate dismissal. The employer has to demonstrate, through progressive discipline, that the employee has been warned and is unable to perform the essential duties of the position. If the employee refuses offered accommodation and if progressive discipline and performance management have been implemented, then disciplinary steps can be taken.

If an employee's drug or alcohol addiction/dependency is interfering with that person's ability to perform the essential duties of the job, the employer must first provide the support necessary to enable that person to undertake a rehabilitation program unless it can be shown that such accommodation would cause undue hardship.

3. Undue Hardship

The employer will be relieved of the duty to accommodate the individual needs of the alcohol or drug addicted/dependent employee if the employer can show, for example, that:

i) the cost of the accommodation would alter the nature or affect the viability of the enterprise; or

ii) notwithstanding accommodation efforts, health or safety risks to workers or members of the public are so serious that they outweigh the benefits of providing equal treatment to the worker with

ENDNOTES

[1] See *Drug and Alcohol Testing in the Workplace*, Report of the ILO Tripartite Experts Meeting (May 1993, Oslo, Norway), cited in Butler et al., *The Drug Testing Controversy: Imperial Oil and Other Lessons* (Carswell, Toronto: 1997) at 5.

[2] As distinct from deterrent value, for which there is no reliable study showing successful outcomes, or for the purposes of monitoring moral values among employees.

[3] Most employers who are subject to U.S. commercial motor vehicle regulations are likely to be under federal jurisdiction under the *Canadian Human Rights Act*. However, even provincially regulated companies that may have only the occasional driver seeking to enter the U.S. are also subject to regulatory requirements for drug and alcohol testing in order to enter the U.S.

[4] There are five social areas covered in the *Code*. These are employment, accommodation (housing), goods services and facilities, membership in vocational associations and contracts.

[5] Letter from Chief Commissioner Keith C. Norton to the Hon. John Baird, Minister of Community and Social Services (unpublished, July 1999). The Commission expressed concern about the Government's announced plans to test welfare recipients for drugs or alcohol.

[6] Section 91 of the *Constitution Act, 1867*.

[7] R.S.C. 1985, c. H-6.

[8] "Handicap" is the term used in the *Code*, but "disability" is the more appropriate term. "Disability" is therefore used in Commission documents except where specific reference to the *Code* requires use of the word "handicap."

[9] "Drug abuse and drug dependence are diseases, illnesses, malfunctions and mental disorders, which can create mental impairment and result in mental disorder and physical disability". *Entrop v. Imperial Oil Ltd.*, Interim Decision #8 Sept. 12, 1996, Decision No. 96-030-I. This

aspect of the ruling was not challenged on appeal to the Court of Appeal. See *Entrop, infra* at note 14.

10 *Ibid.*

11 Adapted from the definition of "substance abuse" in the *Diagnostics and Statistical Manual of Mental Disorders* (American Psychiatric Association, 4th ed., 1994) cited in Entrop #8, *supra* note 9.

12 See, e.g. ss. 5 and 11 of the *Code.*

13 British Columbia (Public Service Employee Relations Commission) v. B.C.G.S.E.U., (1999) 176 D.L.R. (4th) 1 (S.C.C.) [hereinafter Meiorin].

14 Entrop v. Imperial Oil Ltd. (unreported decision of the Ontario Court of Appeal, 21 July 2000).

15 Ibid. at para. 79-82.

16 Ibid.

17 See generally the Commission's Guidelines for Assessing Accommodation Requirements for Persons with Disabilities, in Ontario Human Rights Commission, Human Rights Policy in Ontario (Queen's Printer, Toronto: 1999).

18 See Entrop, supra note 14, citing Meiorin, supra note 13.

19 See Entrop, supra note 14.

20 A copy of the Ontario Human Rights Commission Policy on Employment-Related Medical Information (1996) is available on the Web at www.ohrc.on.ca, through the Commission offices and printed in Human Rights Policy in Ontario, supra note 17.

21 Entrop, supra note 14.

22 Ibid.

SASKATCHEWAN HUMAN RIGHTS COMMISSION

DRUG AND ALCOHOL TESTING (2000)

Why do We Need a Policy?

Drug and alcohol use is an important issue for some employers. They may wish to ensure that no alcohol or illegal drugs are brought into the workplace. Some may wish to ensure that their employees are free from the influence of drugs and alcohol at any time during hours of work. In some jobs, employees whose judgment is impaired by alcohol or drugs may place themselves or others at risk of serious harm. To address these concerns, some employers are implementing drug and alcohol testing programs. Such tests are used to determine the presence of trace amounts of alcohol or drugs in the body. A positive test for drugs or alcohol may lead to discipline or even termination.

Prohibiting employees from possessing, using or being under the influence of illegal drugs or alcohol while in the workplace does not violate the *Saskatchewan Human Rights Code* (the *Code*). However, unnecessary testing and automatic or severe discipline for positive test results may collide with the rights of employees to non-discriminatory treatment. The Commission believes that it would be useful to the public to identify what the *Code* allows and what it prohibits in relation to alcohol and drug testing.

This policy statement constitutes the Commission's interpretation of what is required under the *Code* at the present time. However, the reader should be aware that there are very few court cases as of yet. Many situations that may arise in the normal workday have yet to be explored. How the *Code* will be interpreted in those situations is still open to speculation.

Both drug and alcohol use and steps to curb it are highly contentious and generate strong feelings. Some practices may be considered morally wrong or may be prohibited by collective agreements or other laws. In this policy, the Commission deals only with the effect of the *Code*.

The *Saskatchewan Human Rights Code*

The *Code* establishes that it is public policy in Saskatchewan to recognize the inherent dignity and worth of every person and to provide for equal rights and opportunities without discrimination. In furtherance of this purpose, section 16(1) of the *Code* prohibits employers from discriminating against employees or applicants for employment because of "disability". Boards and Courts have established that dependence or a perceived dependence on drugs or alcohol is a "disability" within the meaning of human rights legislation (*Entrop v. Imperial Oil Ltd.*, [2000] O.J. 2689 (Ont.CA); *Canada (Canadian Human Rights Commission) v. Toronto-Dominion Bank*, [1998] 4 F.C. 205 (F.C.A.)). Therefore, a person cannot be denied employment or terminated simply because of this disability. This does not mean that an employer must tolerate unacceptable work performance. But, as drug or alcohol dependency is a disability, the employer must take reasonable steps to accommodate the employee. For example, if the dependency is interfering with work, the employer may be required to grant a leave of absence so that the employee can participate in a rehabilitation program.

Does Drug and Alcohol Testing Violate the *Code*?

As a general proposition the answer is "yes". One judge stated that a testing policy must necessarily affect those who are drug or alcohol dependant (see the *Toronto-Dominion Bank* case, referred to above). In that case, universal drug testing was unnecessarily implemented by an employer and those who tested positive could eventually be terminated. Positive test results can lead to consequences. Those consequences can have a negative impact on those with a disability.

But the presence of drugs or alcohol in the workplace can also have negative consequences for work performance. Some rules for persons with dependencies may be justified, even if they are discriminatory. Section 16(7) of the *Code* allows discrimination on the basis of disability where the absence of the disability is a reasonable occupational qualification. For example, it is reasonable to prohibit persons who are impaired by alcohol from operating dangerous machines orpublic transportation vehicles.

So When is Drug and Alcohol Allowed?

In what has become known as the *Meiorin* case (*British Columbia (Public Service Employee Relations Commission) v. B.C.G.E.S.U.*, [1999] 3 S.C.R. 3) the Supreme Court of Canada established a three part test which employers must meet to justify employment practices which would otherwise be found to discriminate. These criteria were not formulated specifically in relation disabilities or to drug or alcohol dependency. However, the Ontario Court of Appeal decided in the *Entrop* case, referred to above, that this three-part test establishes when drug and alcohol testing can be justified.

The *Meiorin* Test

The Supreme Court held that in order to justify what would otherwise be discrimination, the employer must show:

1. That the employer adopted the practice for a purpose rationally connected to the performance of the job,
2. That the employer acted honestly and in good faith believing that the practice was necessary for the fulfillment of the work related purpose and
3. That the practice is reasonably necessary for the fulfillment of the work related purpose. In order to meet this last requirement the employer must show:

   a. That the employment practice which has the discriminatory effect does, in fact, achieve the purpose,
   b. That the practice does not go farther than necessary to achieve the purpose and
   c. That, to the point of undue hardship, the employer has attempted to accommodate individuals who suffer a discriminatory effect because of the employment practice.

This is a practical test designed to allow employers to pursue their legitimate fundamental objectives while protecting rights as much as possible and accommodating the needs of employees. Applying this practical test an employer may be able to show in some circumstances that drug or alcohol testing is essential to operate its business enterprise. But, to do so, the employer must meet the *Meiorin* test.

163

What Purposes Might Justify Drug or Alcohol Testing?

The judges in the *Entrop* case accepted that "promoting workplace safety by minimizing the possibility that employees will be impaired by either alcohol or drugs is a legitimate objective". This is the most readily identifiable purpose provided that the employer can show that workplace safety is a real concern. For example, the safety risk of not detecting workers whose performance is impaired by drugs or alcohol is much more serious in a refinery than it is in a bank. This is not to suggest that either the bank or the refinery must tolerate impaired workers. But the bank can deal with poor performance as it occurs, whether caused bydrugs, alcohol or some other factor. In the refinery, it may be vitally important to identify and deal with the impaired employee before there are disastrous consequences. In the refinery situation the employer can establish that minimizing the possibility that the employee might be impaired is rationally connected to the performance of the job. In the financial or service industries this could be considerably more difficult and perhaps impossible.

The cases have not yet established whether there might be other purposes, in relation to drug and alcohol testing, beyond workplace safety. For example, it has not been established whether a legitimate purpose may simply be to prevent the possibility of any use of illegal drugs among employees working in institutions such as schools, prisons, rehabilitation institutes or isolated work camps. However, it is probably true that an employer will not be able to establish any purpose in relation to testing where poor or unacceptable performance can be dealt with effectively after it is discovered as opposed to testing for the presence of drugs or alcohol in the body.

What Does an Employer Have to do to Show Good Faith?

The employer must show that it turned its mind to the business objective and implemented the testing because it believed that testing was necessary to achieve that objective. In the *Entrop* case, referred to above, Imperial Oil was able to show good faith because it consulted widely with its employees and experts in the field of addiction and impairment. It then concluded that drug and alcohol testing was necessary to ensure safety at its refineries. This was sufficient to establish its good faith. By contrast, an employer who simply adopts drug and alcohol testing without seriously considering whether it achieves its objectives may have difficulty establishing good faith.

When can drug and alcohol testing be shown to be reasonably necessary?

There will be no hard and fast rule. The *Meiorin* test focuses on the circumstances of the particular case to establish what is necessary in relation to the specific business purpose. That purpose must be analyzed in relation to what is being tested for, what positions it applies to and when the tests take place. The consequences of a positive test must also be reasonable, in relation to the purpose.

What is Being Tested For

The evidence in the *Entrop* case established that drug testing suffers from a fundamental flaw. It cannot measure present impairment. A positive test only shows past drug use. Furthermore, no tests currently exist which accurately assess the effect of drug use on job performance. Drug testing has not been shown to be effective in reducing drug use, work accidents or work performance problems. It seems clear from this evidence that an employer will have a very difficult time establishing that drug testing is reasonably necessary to minimize the risk of impairment in safety-sensitive jobs. The court in *Entrop* was satisfied that freedom from impairment resulting from either drugs or alcohol is a reasonable job qualification. But the problem with drug testing is that it is not effective in establishing who is impaired and who is not.

On the other hand, the evidence in *Entrop* did establish that alcohol testing is effective. As we all know, a simple breathalyzer test will establish present impairment. Therefore, the Court in *Entrop* found that it was reasonable to randomly test for alcohol impairment in safety sensitive jobs.

It should be noted that the findings in *Entrop* concerning drug and alcohol testing are findings of fact. In the future, if it can be shown that drug testing can be effective in detecting and deterring impairment caused by drugs, then it may be allowed in relation to safety sensitive positions.

Who is Subject to Testing

The testing must be reasonably necessary for the specific positions to which it applies. If the purpose is to detect risks to safety, then it can only be required of those employees who are in safety sensitive positions. Attempts to apply testing to all employees will likely be struck down. Once again, this does not mean that employers are required to tolerate impairment in the work-place. But in most instances, unacceptable work performance caused by impairment can be dealt with when it occurs. In *Entrop*, the Court of Appeal upheld a board's decision that testing was not justifiable for employees who were not in safety sensitive positions.

When Can Testing Take Place

Employers may want to test on a pre-employment basis, randomly, after an incident or as part of agreed upon accommodation. When the testing takes place may be critical in determining whether it can be justified. For example, it may be difficult for an employer to justify any alcohol or drug testing on a pre-employment basis because it is hard to imagine that it accomplishes any objective rationally related to the business of the employer. By definition it does not identify impairment in the workplace. Whether there may be other legitimate employment objectives that require pre-employment testing remains to be seen.

Random testing can be justified in relation to safety sensitive positions. The court in *Entrop* found that random testing for alcohol (but not drugs) could be justified where necessary to detect and deter alcohol impairment.

The importance of detection of impairment in safety sensitive jobs may also justify testing after an incident such as an accident or after what is sometimes described as a near miss. Or there may be other circumstances, such as the smell of alcohol or cannabis smoke that raises a suspicion of drug or alcohol use. If random testing can be justified, it is likely that testing after such incidents can also be justified. Furthermore, testing in situations where there is reason to believe that impairment may be present may be a reasonable and less discriminatory alternative to random drug or alcohol testing.

Finally, testing may be justified in some circumstances as part of a rehabilitation or return to work program. For example, in one case drug testing was held reasonable as a condition of return to work where an employee working in a safety sensitive job was caught several times consuming drugs in the workplace, admitted to a drug dependency, and agreed to participate in a rehabilitation program. This was considered reasonable even though testing might only identify drug use outside work hours (*Re City of Winnipeg and CUPE, Local 500* (1991), 23 L.A.C. (4th) 441).

The Consequences

According to the *Meiorin* test, even where testing is justifiable, the employer still has an obligation to attempt to accommodate the dependent/disabled employee unless to do so would result in an undue hardship. This means that when an employer discovers an impairment it cannot simply impose harsh penalties if it is unnecessary to do so. In the *Entrop* case, the consequence of a positive result after a drug or alcohol test was immediate termination if the employee was in a safety sensitive position. As stated above, the Court allowed the testing to continue, at least in relation to alcohol, but only if the employer considered accommodation in the individual case. In many situations, termination may be too draconian and unnecessary.

A Policy Based on Rights

As is obvious from the above discussion, there is still much uncertainty as to when drug and alcohol testing may be justifiable. However, a few general propositions have been established. The Commission accepts these principles when assessing allegations of discrimination.

- Testing does identify persons with disabilities and does target them for discriminatory treatment. Therefore, in most situations it will not be allowed under the *Code*. This reflects the reality of the work place. Most employers do not consider it necessary to test for drugs and alcohol.
- Testing will only be acceptable in exceptional circumstances that must be justified by the employer in accordance with the criteria established by the Supreme Court of Canada. An employer will have to show that testing achieves a purpose rationally connected to the work, such as preventing impairment in safety sensitive positions, and that it acted in good faith to achieve that purpose. Furthermore, it will have to show that the policy is reasonably necessary in that:
  - It does achieve the purpose,
  - It goes no further than necessary and

- Individual employees are accommodated as far as possible short of undue hardship.

Because drug testing does not determine impairment, it may be justified only in the most unique circumstances. Alcohol testing may be more easily justified in safety sensitive positions.

◆

APPENDIX C

HUMAN RIGHTS COMMISSION
PUBLICATIONS RELATED TO DISABILITY

British Columbia Human Rights Commission
The Duty to Accommodate
Disability — General Interpretation
Dependence on Drugs
Dependence on Alcohol

Canada Human Rights Commission
Policy on HIV/AIDS
Barrier-Free Employers

Manitoba Human Rights Commission
Accommodating Equality: Guidelines

New Brunswick Human Rights Commission
HIV/AIDS Guideline
Pre-employment Inquiries
Guideline on BFOQs and BFQS and the Duty to Accommodate

Ontario Human Rights Commission
Policy on Employment-Related Medical Information
Policy on HIV/AIDS-Related Discrimination

Prince Edward Island Human Rights Commission
Your Rights: Alcohol and Drugs — Testing and Addiction

Index

Absence from work
benefits during disability leave, 36, 38
    monetary, 36
    non-monetary, 36
collective agreement, status under, 37-38
introduction, 35
    length of acceptable absence, 35
last chance agreements, 37
nature of absence, 36-37
    intermittent, 37
    long-term, 36-37
        excessive absenteeism, 37
        prognosis for return to work, 37
replacement, temporary, 38
summary, 38

Accommodate, duty to *See also* **Alberta Human Rights Commission** and **Duty of employee, employer and union**
reasonable accommodation vs. undue hardship, 1-5
    factors not relevant in assessing undue hardship, 2-3
    factors relevant in determining undue hardship, 1, 3-5
        contracts, 4
            collective agreement, 4
            contracting out not permitted, 4
            probationary employee, 4
        costs to employer, 3
        co-workers, interests of, 3
        disruption of operations, 4
        generally, 1
        health and safety, 4
        how much hardship being "undue", 5
            minor inconvenience, far surpassing, 5
            options for employer, 5
            relevant factors varying, 5
        size of business, 3

occupational requirement justified, determining whether, 71
questions considered in applying test, 152, 153
when drug and alcohol testing allowed, 163, 167

Ontario Human Rights Commission
disability and duty to accommodate, 105-142
   accommodate, duty to, 111-125
      duties and responsibilities in accommodation process, 122-125
         confidentiality, 125
            example: AIDS, 125
         employer, 123
         example: bipolar disorder, 124
         example: drug addiction, 123-124
         person with disability, 122-123
         unions, 123
      general principles, 111-115
         individualized accommodation, 112
         integration and full participation, 112-115
            barriers, removing, 114
            design by inclusion, 113-114
            remaining needs, accommodating, 114-115
            United Nations' *Declaration of the Rights of Disabled Persons*, 112-113
         respect for dignity, 111-112
      legal principles, 115-116
         factors considered in assessing accommodation, 116
         individualized accommodation, 115-116
         legal test that must be met, 115, 116
      most appropriate accommodation, 117-125
         alternative work, 119-120
            permanent alternative work, 120-121
            return to work, 121-122
            temporary alternative work, 120
         continuum, accommodation as, 117
         essential duties and current job, 118-119
            "essential" defined, 118
            performance standards, modifying, 118-119
         whether accommodation "appropriate", 117
   discrimination because of disability, *prima facie*, 110-111
      differential treatment, 110
      enumerated ground, 110
      insurance and discrimination, 111

Substance abuse and reasonable accommodation *See also* **Alcohol and drug testing**
accommodating substance abuse, 47-48
    duty of employer and employee, 47-48
        leave of absence to confront alcoholism, 48
        reasonable accommodation where first incident, 47
        reasonable steps by employee to obtain treatment, 47
        strict application of sanctions not acceptable, 47
    undue hardship, assessing, 48
        factors affecting obligation to accommodate, 48
    last chance agreements, 47
alcohol and drug addiction generally, 9
introduction, 43-44
    bona fide occupational requirement that not impaired, 43
on job, 45-46
    disclosure of substance abuse, 45
    testing, 45-46
        human rights commissions, approaches of, 46
        random drug testing, 45, 46
        random testing for alcohol, 45-46
    use of or possession of drugs or alcohol, 46
pre-employment stage, 44-45
    disclosure of substance abuse, 44
    testing, 44-45
        alcohol testing, 44
        drug testing, 44
        policies on pre-employment drug and alcohol testing, 44-45
summary, 49

Suitable alternative employment
assumption of risk, 28-29
    objective assessment of risk, 28-29
    Ontario Human Rights Commission policy, 28
    seriousness of risk and assuming risk, 28
    whether harm to others, 29
collective agreement, 29-30
    mutual duty to facilitate return of disabled employee, 30
    options to accommodate requiring balancing of interests, 30
efficiency, 30-31
generally, 27
part-time work, 28